Twentieth-Century Embroidery in Great Britain to 1939

Constance Howard

B T BATSFORD   LONDON

Acknowledgment

Firstly I would like to thank Thelma M Nye for her patience, as the book has taken some time to write. Everyone who has contributed, those who have lent photographs, supplied information and the biographies, have helped to make the book possible, and I give them my grateful thanks. I greatly appreciate the help given to me by the textile staff of the Victoria and Albert Museum, the Costume Study Centre, Bath, and the Art Gallery and Museum, Glasgow. I am grateful to the Convent of St Mary, Wantage, for advice and supplying photographs or allowing them to be taken; to Miss Chrissie White for sending me information and photographs; and to Maurice H Prior who compiled the index.

I wish to thank the following who photographed examples of embroidery for me, for their willingness to fetch and carry work: John Hunney (Nos. 70, 71, 75, 77, 79, 80, 94, 97, 108, 109, 120, 123, 130, 134); May Miller (No. 17); Nick Nicholson (Frontispiece, Nos. 2–6, 12–16, 19, 20, 23, 24, 26, 30, 32, 33, 36–38, 47, 48, 56, 57, 59, 60, 66, 67, 69, 72, 74, 76, 81, 82, 83, 91, 93, 98–100, 102–106, 110, 112, 113, 115, 118, 119, 121, 122, 138, 144, 149, colour plates 1, 8, 9); Paul Scott (68, 90, 107, 127, colour plate 5).

Lastly I would like to say that I am most grateful to my daughter, Charlotte, who has given me a great deal of advice when checking proofs.

First published 1981
Reprinted 1982
Reprinted 1985

ISBN 0 7134 3942 4

Filmset in Monophoto Times New Roman by
Servis Filmsetting Ltd, Manchester
and printed in Great Britain by
Anchor Brendon Ltd
Tiptree, Essex
for the publishers
B T Batsford Ltd
4 Fitzhardinge Street
London W1H 0AH

Contents

Introduction

The history of embroidery and costume should be studied within the social and political context of the countries in which they flourished. The wealth or poverty, the strategic position in relation to other countries, the power of the Court, are all factors which help to determine the quality of life within a country and subsequently the importance of its artists and craftsmen and their contribution to the cultural scene.

The Court and the Church were great patrons of the visual arts, which, before the advent of books, were a means of communication to an illiterate population. The power and the munificence of these patrons were expressed in the magnificent decoration within their buildings and on their persons – richly embroidered hangings and articles for the household, ecclesiastical vestments and costume for religious and civic occasions. Frequently royal robes were given as gifts to the Church, or in the case of ecclesiastical vestments of the *Opus Anglicanum* period, as gifts to foreign dignitaries. The luxurious materials elaborately embroidered in metal threads and silks, which constituted the court costumes of a sophisticated society, were in contrast to the colourful but coarser embroidery worked on woollen or linen fabrics by a peasant population whose crafts were limited by their environment, and by indigenous climatic conditions.

England had no embroidered peasant costume as did other European countries; her insularity led to the development of her own resources and during the mediaeval period England became famous for woollens and worsteds. These were unpatterned and so were often decorated with embroidery. Rich Italian brocades, velvets and silks, gold and silver threads and pure silk threads were imported for the sumptuous embroideries executed by the Guild of Embroiderers, among these being the *Opus Anglicanum* vestments of the mid-thirteenth to the mid-fourteenth centuries, carried out in London in the professional workshops for export.

Embroidery for the Church declined after the Black Death in 1349, although inventories suggest that domestic embroidery continued to flourish. Religious suppression by Henry VIII, with the dissolution of the monasteries, led to much embroidery being destroyed, although some, fortunately, was hidden and

About 1936 – Rebecca Crompton. 'Jewelled Swan', 54 in. × 36 in. (137 cm × 91 cm). Off-white fur fabric is applied onto a cream fur fabric background. The swan is in cream satin with cream net stripes. Its head is in silver brocade, couched in silver 'plate' and ric-rac braid. Cream satin circles with cream silk chain stitch, white raised buttonhole circles, cream tweed flames couched in silk and silver metallic fabric leaves are applied. The oval frame is surrounded by five rows of white opaque sequins, while the background trellis is in white sequins. Unravelled white piping cord with silver thread and cream silk makes frond-like shapes round the frame. Silver stars and studs are scattered within the oval. The base of water is dark cream fabric woven with silver thread, with strips of cream satin overlaid with cream net, applied between the circles of slightly padded cream satin sewn down with stars. The embroidery was exhibited at the fiftieth exhibition of the Arts and Crafts Exhibition Society in 1938. The reviewer, Mrs Platt, described it as 'the product of a fairy godmother'. *By courtesy of Madame Sheeta*

therefore saved. On the other hand Henry VIII and Elizabeth I both loved finery, and there was an upsurge of domestic embroidery which has been unsurpassed in inventiveness and technique. Its richness, with jewel-encrusted patterns in gold thread, its raised stitches and relief effects on backgrounds crowded with sequins, produced a splendour not to be equalled again.

The end of the sixteenth century was marked by adventure and discovery, with the expansion of trade routes to the East, with intellectual attainments in fields previously unexplored, and with more communication between countries. Foreign influences noticeably affected styles and techniques of embroidery during the seventeenth century.

Around 1600 the East India Company was formed. English embroideries were exported to India where they had some influence on the design of the embroideries of that country. During the latter half of the seventeenth century, the Jacobean style of embroidery was derived mainly from Indian palampores imported to Britain. Hangings, bed covers, curtains and other household textiles were decorated while costume remained comparatively unembroidered.

The predominant Oriental influence of the eighteenth century was Chinese. Fine silk embroidery featuring peonies, pagodas and exotic birds was one of the styles. Costume as well as domestic articles was now embroidered, sometimes elaborately.

Until the middle of the eighteenth century, when the Industrial Revolution changed the British way of life, there were few epoch-making events to have any strong effect on embroidery. With the invention of machinery the textile industry was revolutionised and the agricultural workers, and many craftsmen, migrated from the rural to the urban areas in the hope of obtaining better wages. Patterned fabrics began to appear, obviating the necessity for embroidery as decoration which, with the cost of labour, became prohibitive in England. When embroidery was required, garments were sent to France or as far away as China to be worked. The elaborate waistcoats and dresscoats worn by men towards the end of the century were sometimes embroidered in France where skilled labour was still available at a reasonable price.

With the growth of manufacture, items which had been beyond the reach of all but the rich became cheaper. Embroidery machines produced patterned ribbons, machine-made laces appeared, plain fabrics were printed with patterns. Embroidery therefore became superfluous as a way of decorating costume and instead was a means of occupying the time of the bored wives of the wealthy woollen and cotton manufacturers. The spread of instructions in cheap magazines on 'how to do it' tended to popularise the craft as a 'hobby' for anyone with nothing better to do. Berlin woolwork dominated a greater part of the nineteenth century but fancy work and 'art' needlework took precedence towards its closing years. The emphasis on technical achievement rather than on ideas can, in retrospect, be seen as one of the reasons for the rejection of embroidery by the art world. In the 1880s there were signs of a growing interest in the craft movements and in art when various societies were formed. Despite the vicissitudes through which embroidery has passed, it has emerged during the twentieth century from being a hobby to its present status as a serious art.

The twentieth century is the most amazing of all centuries for its technological inventions, educational advancements, and the general raising of social standards. A greater awareness of the arts and their value to the community has been promoted by exhibitions, free lectures in museums, radio, and later by television. Likewise, the therapeutic values of art and craft have been recognised. Attitudes to crafts have changed considerably through the century and, where possible, I have quoted contemporary opinions on exhibitions, on individual artists and their work, and their thoughts on current standards of embroidery. From some opinions, strongly expressed in the earlier decades of the century, it would appear that design was a weak point while technique was of prime importance in English embroidery. Scotland seems to have been ahead in design and the appreciation of the aesthetics of the craft.

The background to twentieth-century embroidery

The Great Exhibition, 1851

In order to understand the development of embroidery in the twentieth century and how late nineteenth- and early twentieth-century attitudes to design were merged it is necessary to have some knowledge of nineteenth-century attainments. A brief resumé from 1851, when the great Exhibition was held on the site of what is now the Victoria and Albert Museum, South Kensington, London, seems a good starting point for the understanding of the growth of the craft.

Prince Albert, the Prince Consort, devised the Exhibition, the aim of which was to show the world what could be achieved in the progressive age of industry. Goods and raw materials from all over the world were assembled to demonstrate the highest technical skills and aesthetic tastes in the arts and in industry. Craftsmen excelled themselves in their endeavours to produce their best and most ingenious works, but, sadly, these were often tasteless and vulgar. Embroidery featured strongly in this Exhibition. Among the exhibits were a collar worked by an Irish peasant, three examples of patchwork by men, a copy of a print of Lincoln Cathedral in fine black silk, and a great deal of Berlin woolwork, often of a pictorial nature; biblical subjects were popular, Leonardo da Vinci's 'Last Supper' being copied six times in this technique. (See page 18.)

Carpets were also exhibited, many made up of squares worked in cross stitch then sewn together. Machine embroidery was also on show, worked on the hand-operated industrial machine, produced by the firm of Henry Houldsworth who had purchased the rights of the first embroidery machine in 1829 and was foremost in this field of embroidery in England until the 1870s.

Deterioration of the craft

Embroidery during the middle of the century had reached a low ebb as a skilled, creative craft, caused mainly by women's popular magazines which showed diagrams of patterns and gave instruction on 'how to do it' techniques. This was not new as magazines appeared in the eighteenth century with such advice, but the cheap magazines proliferated from the mid nineteenth century, most of them showing little artistic merit. Thread manufacturers issued stitch charts, and 'easy to make' publications appeared, which became more numerous later in the century, advocating the sole use of a particular brand of thread for the effects described. Most of these magazines gave suggestions for the adornment of accessories, for costume, and for the home, all easy to accomplish, taking little time or effort and so reducing a once skilled craft to a facile occupation.

As the Industrial Revolution progressed, a wealthy merchant class emerged which could afford the luxury of servants. This meant that the wives of these merchants had a great deal of leisure which they occupied in embroidering knick-knacks.

Berlin woolwork

Berlin woolwork became the most fashionable craze of the mid-1850s. Although it started in the early part of the century, this type of work on canvas now overshadowed all other forms of embroidery. Little skill was required in working from printed charts or from patterns already coloured in on squared paper. Brilliantly coloured, soft wools were used often mixed with silk and beads. Designs during the 1850s were mainly floral, with exotic birds. Upholstered furniture in canvas work was popular in cross or tent stitch but by the 1860s smaller articles, such as cushion covers or stool tops, were embroidered. Pictures too tended to disappear with the discovery of a greater number of stitches and different materials. Patterns became geometric rather than floral, and beads continued in popularity, but by the 1870s Berlin woolwork was disappearing (pages 18, 19, 20).

Coggeshall lace

An embroidered lace which reached its peak about 1851 should be mentioned. This was Essex lace, made in Coggeshall, using a tambour hook to work chain stitch on machine-made net, described as round but probably hexagonal as compared with the diamond mesh used for Limerick lace. The shapes within the chain stitch outlines were often filled in with delicate needle-run patterns, although fine chain stitch patterns were worked too. Designs were usually floral, or with semi-geometric shapes combined with trailing stems, leaves and flowers. Until 1859 the craft flourished, but then fluctuated and finally, with the introduction of machine-made laces, the industry dwindled as there was more demand for the cheaper manufactured articles which were produced in quantity.

White embroidery

Also introduced during the 1850s but continuing until the end of the century was broderie anglaise, which consisted of patterns made by small oval leaf shapes cut out and whipped or buttonholed round the edges, with eyelet holes similarly worked (pages 21, 27). This technique was imitated later by machine.

Other forms of whitework were revivals of embroidered laces, grouped under the general term of guipure work, some being based on the Venetian padded laces of the seventeenth century, others on the cutwork known as richelieu or renaissance, in which much of the ground fabric was cut away, the floral patterns being held together with bars, plainly whipped or with picots (pages 37, 47, 59).

Fancy work

In so-called 'fancy work' mixed techniques were often put together indiscriminately, embroidery being combined with knitting and crochet, as well as painting. Its zenith was during the 1880s. Some of its facets are described in *The Housewife's Treasury of Domestic Information* by Mrs Beeton who lists 'fancy work' within the category of embroidery, with Berlin woolwork, broderie anglaise, crewel work, appliqué, netting, guipure, net darning and braid laces, as well as straw plaiting. Appliqué was fashionable during the 1850s for the decoration of costume and later for hangings and other household articles. Contrasts of texture in one colour were popular and velvet with satin or other rich fabrics was used for the black garments worn after Prince Albert's death, the applied edges being covered with braid or beads, often jet. Mrs Beeton says that for dress, black net frequently formed the foundation, and on this, black cloth or cashmere was applied with the edges outlined in black braid. According to her the fashion soon came to an end, principally because of the meaningless vulgarity of the patterns. Braids were popular during the nineteenth century, particularly in the 1850s, when they were used to decorate costume and some household articles. Later, ribbons, fancy braids and Russian braids were combined with embroidery.

Societies and schools

The Society of Arts, inaugurated in 1754, held public exhibitions of crafts and in 1855 established a system of examinations for artisans to encourage the raising of craft standards.

In the hope of training designers who could help to raise the standards of the mass-produced factory goods, schools of design were formed as early as 1837, with the Government School of Design at Somerset House, and in 1857 the

National Art Training School at South Kensington; but these schools did not affect the standards of crafts until a much later date when embroidery, with other handcrafts, was introduced to them.

Arts and Crafts Movement

Following on from the Great Exhibition of 1851 what became known as the Arts and Crafts Movement evolved, with William Morris, a trained architect and painter, a prime instigator in the attempt to raise the standards of the arts and crafts in the country. It was realised that the skills of the country were not being developed, and enlightened people were beginning to do something about this situation. In the mid-1850s there were signs of change and in 1854 the Ladies' Ecclesiastical Embroidery Society was formed to give advice on and to design church furnishings. Miss Blencowe and Miss Street (the sister of George Street, an architect who designed ecclesiastical buildings and embroideries (page 21)) were the leading figures. During the late 1850s a group of artists and designers met together with a similar idea in mind, to discuss craft and design standards as these had sunk lower with increased factory production. Among them were George Street and Philip Webb, both architects, and William Morris who had worked for Street, but in 1861 opened his own firm of Morris, Marshall and Faulkner. Morris practised many crafts including dyeing his own yarns and weaving them into tapestries. He also made embroidered hangings. He used vegetable dyes for all his yarns, although synthetic dyes were manufactured after the discovery in 1857 by W H Perkins of mauveine, the first dye developed from coal-tar. These synthetic dyes were in the beginning crude in colour, but by the 1870s became more subtle in quality. William Morris was fanatical in that he wished to return entirely to handmade crafts as in the mediaeval period, believing that the machine was responsible for the poor results now in evidence; in fact it was a lack of understanding by artists as to what machines could do, as they were untrained in designing for machine production, so manufactured goods remained low in standard.

Edward Burne-Jones designed large embroidered hangings for Morris's firm, which were worked in outline stitch. He was reputed to have drawn the figures according to ideas suggested by Morris, not a figure draughtsman. Morris designed wallpapers during the 1870s. These influenced his embroidery designs which sometimes became repetitive, although his portières and coverlets varied in style. (Page 23.)

Catherine Holiday, who interpreted many of his patterns, used her own colour schemes with success (page 21).

Church embroidery

George Frederick Bodley, another noted church architect, designed embroideries for the Ecclesiastical Embroidery Society and for his own buildings (page 52), as well as for the firm of Watts and Co which was started by him and a group of architects who were unable to find anyone to carry out their designs for ecclesiastical embroideries. A great interest in church work was developing during the second half of the century, stimulated by the Gothic Revival in which A W Pugin, earlier in the nineteenth century, was a key figure.

Designs during the 1850s were mainly mediaeval in style but during the next decade they became more in keeping with the period.

In 1862 The Great International Exhibition showed examples of embroidery by well-known ecclesiastical furnishers which led to an enthusiasm for the designing of banners until the end of the century. Embroideries now showed an angular quality in design. Gold thread and rich fabrics were employed, one of the chief exponents being W Curtis Brangwyn, an architect (page 22).

In 1863 the Ladies' Ecclesiastical Embroidery Society combined with the Wantage Church Needlework Association which was composed of Exterior Sisters and Friends of St Mary's House, Wantage, Berkshire (*Victorian Embroidery*, Barbara Morris page 88). This group undertook all types of ecclesiastical embroidery (pages 21, 24, 25).

A number of groups formed during the 1870s and 1880s had repercussions on the craft of embroidery, helping to give it greater stature than previously.

The Royal School of Art Needlework

In 1872 the Royal School of Art Needlework was promoted by Lady Welbey and Mrs Dolbry 'to give amateurs and gentlewomen instructions in fine needlework and to reproduce from good designs the old English needlework on handmade linen, so often spoken of as Jacobean work'. There were six workers initially and the many orders meant a move from Sloane Street to larger premises. Historical embroideries were copied faithfully, the work produced being of superb technical proficiency but lacking in originality or life. The School worked commissions and by the end of 1875 had increased considerably in size and moved to Exhibition Road. The School was separated into departments, with a head and an assistant in each. The general workroom executed a variety of types of embroidery, another one was devoted to appliqué and goldwork, while the 'artistic room' carried out crewel embroideries from the designs of the artists employed by the School. A fourth department produced work which could be finished by the amateur embroiderer at home. Exhibitions of historic needlework were held during the latter part of the century which encouraged the study and, incidentally, the copying of the old work. In 1873 an exhibition was held at the South Kensington Museum, now the Victoria and Albert Museum, in the Liverpool Art Club in 1875, and in the Edinburgh Museum of Science and Art in 1877.

In 1875, Lady Alford, in a speech given at the opening of the new premises of the Royal School of Art Needlework, advocated that 'all embroidery should be as natural as possible . . . nothing should be left to the imagination of the stitcher . . . each must copy . . . the design which should always be placed before her'.

Art needlework using crewel wools, silks and metal threads for surface stitchery on linen, satin and other fabrics, now tended to overshadow Berlin woolwork. This type of embroidery was popular for some time, interest in it continuing into the twentieth century. It was prompted by the Royal School of Art Needlework which now asked well-known architects and designers to produce ideas for them, which they executed. William Morris, Edward Burne-Jones, G F Bodley and Selwyn Image were among these as well as **Walter Crane**, an illustrator and painter of great versatility. The latter designed figurative hangings on a large scale and smaller panels for the School, and was prolific in his output (page 26). His designs and those of other well known artists were exhibited at the Centennial Exhibition in Philadelphia in 1876. These embroideries so impressed the Americans that they opened 'art needlework' schools forthwith in many parts of the country. Walter Crane continued to design for the School as did the other artists.

An artist working in Scotland at this time, probably inspired by the historic embroideries, was **Phoebe Traquair** who had a brief training as a painter and for some time drew fish skeletons and other natural forms for her husband, the Keeper of the Natural History Department of the Museum of Science and Art, Edinburgh. She was an extremely versatile artist and received commissions for mural decoration, book illustration and illumination and became, as well as an embroiderer, an enameller and jeweller. Early extant work dates from the end of the 1870s, and includes one cloth dated 1879 in the Victoria and Albert Museum. (See page 24.) The style is reminiscent of the art needlework at that time in vogue. Her later work was more personal, although a tea cosy of 1880 shows a design of flowers and leaves similar to the Greek embroidery of Yannina, with the traditional colours and forms. Her most important work was done between 1895 and 1902: a fourfold screen of allegorical figures, one filling each panel, depicting the four 'spiritual stages in the life of man' as described in Pater's *Imaginary Portraits*. The ground of linen is covered completely with stitchery in silk and gold threads. It was first exhibited at the Arts and Crafts Exhibition in 1903 and in 1904 in the United States, at the St Louis International Exhibition. At the end of the century she was well known in the Arts and Crafts Movement in Scotland.

The copying of historic embroideries was fostered by a revival of interest in mediaevalism, through William Morris and his desire to return to the concept of crafts worked entirely by hand.

In 1875 the Ladies' Work Society was founded in Sloane Street, with the idea of helping gentlewomen in poor circumstances to earn their livings; also to raise the standard of needlework. Conservation was undertaken: old, worn embroideries were remade into new articles, an example quoted by Barbara Morris in her book *Victorian Embroidery* being 'a badly worn ecclesiastical vestment which might be remounted as a screen'.

By the mid-1870s schools of art needlework were opened in various parts of England and embroideries on wool, linen, crash or serge worked in crewel wools became the fashion, with designs often copied from the crewel work of the seventeenth century; silk was used too, sometimes on velvet, the chief stitch being outline, or an uneven stem stitch called 'crewel stitch', or occasionally long and short stitch which followed the shapes of the design, sometimes left in outline, sometimes filled in. Colours were dull, patterns mainly floral, with such 'aesthetic' flowers as the iris, sunflower and lily usually 'faithfully copied in natural colours'. A long list of floral designs for sale from the School of Art Needlework was issued. Birds too remained popular but were English rather than oriental in type: cranes and peacocks rather than parrots and smaller birds such as ducks or swallows. Figurative subjects were favourites, allegorical and classical, often combined with lettering and worked as panels for screens, while smaller embroideries were made into fire screens, among which were the so called 'Jacobean designs' taken from the seventeenth century.

Commercial enterprise

William Briggs and Co Ltd

At this time supplies for embroidery and needlework flourished. Information from the firm of William Briggs and Co Ltd says that letters patent were granted in 1874 to John Briggs, Richard Hudson and Henry Grimshaw acknowledging their invention of the hot-iron transfer. The name 'Penelope' was registered in 1886 when the firm began to sell items for embroidery, including silk threads. Their premises in Manchester expanded and, in parallel with the transfer business, they developed traced needlework patterns which flourished with the increased interest in stitchery rather than in Berlin woolwork. However, embroidery on canvas continued in popularity, worked on a single thread mesh called 'Tammy-cloth' in white, cream or écru, with stitchery in white knitting cotton in geometric patterns. This was known as French canvas work.

There was a craze for cross stitch embroidery in the 1880s and William Briggs and Co Ltd invented a fabric which had perforated patterns of holes made by machine which could be worked more quickly than by counting threads.

Liberty and Company

A believer in the Arts and Crafts movement was Arthur Lazenby Liberty, who had founded the firm of Liberty and Company in 1875. He dealt particularly with eastern silks which became popular after the Japanese woodcut print had been introduced to Europe. He hoped to influence the public by showing only carefully-selected goods in his shop and also by staging exhibitions which included beautiful textiles, such as embroideries and laces from various sources. A costume section opened in 1884, where garments were hand-embroidered. These were often worked very simply, but the more elaborate metal thread embroidery, beadwork and smocking were also popular means of embellishing gowns. An art needlework section received designs from well-known embroiderers, while printed fabrics by Thomas Wardle's firm were sold in the shop.

Leek Embroidery Society

In Leek, Staffordshire, a group of ecclesiastical embroiderers was working together during the early seventies and in 1879 several of the ladies of this group became members of a small but influential body known as The Leek Embroidery Society, founded in Staffordshire by Elizabeth Wardle whose husband owned a silk mill. He was an authority on dyeing and silk printing and had assisted William Morris in his early dyeing experiments. The group embroidered in silk and gold threads on plain and printed tussore silk, on velvets and on velveteens, and on

Thomas Wardle's woven silks. They carried out their own ecclesiastical designs to high standards and were commissioned by architects to work designs by well-known artists. Ellen Masters in her *Book of Art Needlework* says:

'Many of the Leek velveteens are splendid in design, and often display flowing scrolls, admirably suited for enrichment with needlework. The silks are generally printed in "all-over" designs and find few rivals as portières, where the portion of the pattern that is in the middle or fold of the curtain is left plain, the design for a distance of some inches within the edges being richly worked over with silks and gold thread to form a border.'

Another description says that the richness of the Leek embroidery was obtained by patterns placed close together, with very little background showing. The floss silks and the Japanese gold outlining these patterns produced a sumptuous quality (pages 28, 61).

A project which became well known at the time was the making of a full-sized facsimile of the Bayeaux Tapestry by the Leek Embroidery Society. The idea to reproduce this may have been conceived by Elizabeth Wardle after seeing photographs of the work in the Victoria and Albert Museum, or she may have seen it in Bayeux; it is not clear, but the tapestry was copied between 1885 and 1886 by a group of 35 women. Thomas Wardle dyed the yarns to the exact shades required. When complete in the mid 1880s it went on tour and was eventually bought by the Reading Museum and Art Gallery.

Among the many work societies set up in England during the 1880s was an offshoot from the Royal School of Art Needlework, the Decorative Needlework Society, founded in 1880, whose aim was to produce a high standard of work at a moderate cost. Repairs were also undertaken. It was believed by these societies that embroidery as an art could be revived only by a proper study of historic work and from the seventies onwards this was undertaken by most of these societies.

In Scotland one of the most important groups was the Wemyss Castle School of Embroidery started by Lady Lilian Wemyss and Miss Wemyss to give occupation to the poor in the East Fife area. The School carried out all types of embroidery, becoming a flourishing concern.

Aesthetic dress

An enlightened group of women started a revolt against the uncomfortable costume of the late 1870s, which led to the aesthetic movement and dress reform. Tight, uncomfortable garments were discarded in favour of loosely flowing gowns, embroidered in crewel wools in the art needlework styles of the day. Although ridiculed and called the 'greenery yallery' movement, this freer style of dress had some influence on sports costumes; but there were protests from embroiderers that the decoration on the garments was out of place, old fashioned and too obvious. With the looser gown, smocking became fashionable and an established means of decorating dress. Children's clothes had smocked yokes while women's garments were generally smocked at the waist, the sleeves and across the yoke. Weldons, who published magazines on embroidery, knitting, crochet and allied crafts issued patterns and instructions on smocking which were in favour almost to the end of the century. For smarter occasions beads were sewn into honeycomb patterns.

During the 1880s drawn threadwork became popular, a revival of an earlier craze, but it was now combined with cut work and coarser than previously. Evenly woven linens were used for the embroidery, also linen gauze and muslin. Designs were geometric, and were used for decoration on household linens and garments.

Patchwork

Patchwork had been made since the beginning of the century, cotton fabrics being used for the early examples, usually quilts sewn in traditional patterns, either pieced or applied. Later, rich fabrics such as silks and velvets were used, often with added embroidered decoration. Mrs R N Norris in Stratford-upon-Avon made a series of what could be called a combination of patchwork and fabric collage pictorial panels, completely personal in style, one being dated 1876.

Crazy patchwork, so called, was very popular in the 1880s and consisted of small pieces of fabric, often velvets and silks, put together indiscriminately, the textures and colours mixed. Various stitches joined these pieces, many of which were embellished further with embroidery in a variety of motifs such as butterflies, birds, small flowers and patterns in stitches. Quilts, cushion covers and dress accessories were fashioned in this patchwork and by using woollen scraps sewn to a background with the edges embroidered together, cheap quilts were made

Ruskin lace

A localised industry began in Langdale in the Lake District in 1883, when The Home Arts and Industries Association was started, promoting various classes, embroidery becoming a subject soon after its commencement. Mrs Pepper, inspired by Ruskin, revived the art of hand-weaving linen which she then embellished with embroidery. The industry flourished with the help of Albert Fleming, a friend of Ruskin. Italian linen embroideries were a source of ideas as were those from the Greek Islands and the examples produced by the workers became known as Greek lace embroidery or Ruskin lace. Groups of threads were whipped into firm bars embellished with buttonhole stitch, and pattern darning gave a coarse texture to the backgrounds of the geometric designs. The technique had an attractive, lacy effect (page 28).

Promotion of the Arts and Crafts Movement

Various societies interested in the promotion of the Arts and Crafts Movement were formed during the 1880s. Artists and craftsmen began to meet together to initiate groups for the promotion and betterment of the arts and crafts in their area. In 1882 The Century Guild was the first to be founded under the auspices of Arthur Mackmurdo, who designed textiles and furniture and was a versatile artist and an architect of considerable talent. Selwyn Image and many well-known craftsmen were members of this Guild, and also of the Art Workers' Guild, which was started in 1884 by a group of five young architects. The aim was to encourage meetings between artists and craftsmen, so that they should understand one another's skills. It became a thriving body of artists, architects, and craftsmen, interested in all branches of arts and crafts. Walter Crane and Lewis F Day were members, the two of them often collaborating over projects.

Through these groups and the general Arts and Crafts Movement, magazines on arts and crafts appeared; among these *The Studio, Arts and Crafts* and *The Hobby Horse* were prominent. Their aims were to spread information and ideas among craftsmen and to encourage the handmade crafts in order to counteract the mass produced factory article with its lack of individuality or artistic merit.

Commercial enterprise in the 1880s

According to an undated catalogue (but later than 1965), a firm whose aim was 'to create beautiful furnishing fabrics', in an age when design was suffering from mechanisation, was that of Arthur H Lee and Sons of Birkenhead. The firm was founded in Warrington in 1888, moving to Birkenhead in 1908. Arthur Lee's aim was to produce furnishing fabrics of quality, both in design and workmanship. Reproductions of antique tapestries and embroideries suitable for upholstery were made, many of these hand-worked, using wools specially dyed for individual pieces of work. For their canvas embroideries a variety of hard-wearing stitches was used, such as tent, cross and gobelin. On woollen garments some areas were left unstitched. Embroidery entirely in one stitch was favoured. The firm was noted for its crewel embroidery; their 'Jacobean' work being carried out in unshaded wools, while other works were stitched in shaded threads. The fabric was a damask linen or 'Jacobean' twill, long and short stitch being employed for the main part of the embroidery. Designs were adapted from seventeenth- and eighteenth-century embroideries and tapestries. These ranged from simple sprig motifs to complicated figurative subjects, adapted to the widths of the woven fabrics. In 1903 a branch of the firm opened in the USA, and other branches opened later in other countries.

15

William Morris in 1888 became the first president of the Arts and Crafts Exhibition Society which was strongly supported by Walter Crane and Lewis F Day among others. Morris, with his fanatical reaction against machine-made goods, his abhorrence of industry and his energy in promoting the hand crafts had a wide influence, although his efforts to raise the standards of embroidery in this country were not immediately appreciated. The discovery of Japanese woodcut prints had some impact in England during the 1860s but did not influence embroidery until the establishment of art needlework, when floss silks were introduced and metal threads, including the imported Japanese gold, became fashionable. Simple shapes appliquéd in subdued colours were reminiscent of the flat areas of the prints and were often outlined in gold thread, these outlines giving an oriental quality to work during the last years of the nineteenth century. The import of Japanese and Chinese embroideries by Liberty fostered an interest in oriental embroideries. The influence of a new style, emerging in the 1880s, was also evident in the use of plant forms in design: flowers such as the lily, sunflower and tulip were used, with elongated and undulating stems. (Colour plate 1).

Art Nouveau

This style had a gradual birth and was the culmination of many influences. It originally stemmed from William Blake's symbolism, and was developed through the Pre-Raphaelite Brotherhood, the Arts and Crafts Movement and by certain artists, including Walter Crane and Christopher Dresser, a brilliant English designer. By the end of the century the style was known as Art Nouveau, gaining its name from Samuel Bing, whose shop in Paris in 1895 was called 'L'Art Nouveau'. By the end of the century this name was accepted for the style in which long writhing stems supported flowers and buds, often with curling foliage. Particular characteristics evolved in different countries. Several artists became noted for their individual approaches to design in this manner. The fashion for designs derived from plants and flowers was due partly to the work of William Morris. (Colour plate 2 and pages 23, 51, 60, 61, 63.)

In 1885 when William Morris became too busy to take a personal interest in all the concerns of his firm, J N Dearle, the chief designer, continued to follow closely his style of decorative work, while **May Morris** his daughter, took charge of the embroidery. She showed an individual approach but she pursued the Morris tradition in basing her design on plant forms. In 1893 she published *Decorative Needlework*, the first book on embroidery to advocate drawing from nature and other sources as a basis of original design. Her ideas expressed what might be termed 'the modern outlook'.

May Morris was a hard worker and a good teacher. Owing to the time given to the embroidery workrooms in her father's firm and later when she was editing his papers, she had little time left for the pursuit of her own work. She was a good critic of exhibitions and had sound ideas on design saying that in embroidery 'stitches must be interesting, also spaces, restraint tells more than profusion'.

Some of the advice in her book was far seeing and contained important points in learning to design for embroidery from natural forms. She said:

'The most important element in successful work is the choice of design . . . inferior work can be tolerated for the sake of the design, if that is good, . . . excellent work on a worthless design must be cast as labour lost. . . The modern tendency . . . is to copy some spray or bough directly from nature and to lay it down haphazard on the surface to be ornamented; a few stray petals or a broken leaf and a caterpillar about elsewhere without rhyme or reason; this is then called "quaint" design. No attempted copying of the painter's art in such dissimilar and insufficient materials is permissible. The first thing a designer will do is to go to the natural growths . . . studying their infinite variety and beauty. . . His own work should merely recall nature, not absolutely copy it. . . . Whatever growth is chosen as a model will thus be represented . . . but translated. . . . Therefore not to draw a line you do not understand . . . let every form you put on paper be something, explain something.'

She then goes on to explain with great clarity elements in design such as contrast, repetition, line and colour.

Mrs Beeton advised that 'the practice of drawing and of needlework should go hand in hand. Ornamental designs and outlines of natural flowers may be copied and at the same time, the worker should endeavour to make drawings from natural leaves and flowers.' An awareness of the need for original ideas was evident from her remarks and those of May Morris.

Ellen Masters in her book *The Gentlewoman's Book of Art Needlework*, 1892, made some pertinent remarks too, saying that:

'The designs reproduced in needlework have undergone considerable improvement of late years, alongside that in the material and threads upon them; but the scarcity of originality is as strongly marked now as in the early days of this nineteenth-century renaissance. The workers are, for the most part quite content to follow slavishly in the footsteps of old designers. . . . An exception is to be found at the Royal School of Art Needlework, the Leek Embroidery Society, the Decorative Needlework Society, and several similar establishments where the designs used are often prepared by artists of high position and well-known excellence. . . . To a connoisseur a piece of work designed, traced and executed from beginning to end by the embroideress herself is, even if faulty, possessed of far more interest. . . . and far more individuality than such as is sold already designed and planned. No worker who has once felt the intense pleasure there is in originating a design . . . will ever again remain satisified with executing the mere stitchery alone. . . . In such work as this the design has a far better chance of success than when the draughtsman and embroiderers work quite independently of one another . . . Amateur designers . . . believe that their aim and object should be to produce with their needles a picture of flowers, birds or fruits so realistically as to elicit admiration from all beholders.'

There was an awareness now that design and drawing were important if embroidery was to be thought of as an art as well as a craft; but Ellen Masters, who was conversant with the printed silks of Thomas Wardle, felt that 'The notion of following the pattern upon a printed fabric is by no means to be despised by a worker who doesn't possess . . . artistic skill to enable her to prepare her own designs.'

Machine embroidery – the trade

Machine embroidery using the trade machines was taught at the Macclesfield School of Embroidery, opened in 1889 by the owner of a silk-weaving mill, while machine embroidery on leather was produced by the firm of Marshall and Rae of Nottingham for upholstery. A number of domestic machines of different makes were now in use, although the best known were those made by Singer seen first at the 1851 Exhibition. In their workrooms during the 1890s some remarkable embroidered pictures were produced, often copied from postcards with subjects from well-known paintings, portraits, landscapes and seascapes. These were stitched on domestic machines with fixed needles, the fabric being moved to give zigzag, satin and other stitches. Great patience and technical skill were necessary when embroidering these pictures, some of which were produced by highly skilled embroiderers working in their own homes.

Beadwork

As a trade, embroidery by hand or machine was considered a very low-grade occupation and conditions under which embroiderers worked were poor; lighting was inadequate, space was cramped, wages were poor – in fact they worked in sweat shops. Bead decoration on costume was fashionable, particularly the use of French jet or purple glass on black fabric, after Queen Victoria went into mourning for Prince Albert (page 27). The application of the beads was by hand, then by means of a bamboo hook. At the beginning of the twentieth century an invention in France which modified the Cornely chain stitch machine made it possible to sew on beads by machine, thus reducing the time factor. Wages remained inadequate.

Descriptions of beadwork on garments do not mention embroidery, other than machine-made broderie anglaise, as lace was now the favourite means of embellishment. One description of 1894 (*The Woman at Home*) is of 'a charming jacket from Messrs Jay's showrooms', made of pale heliotrope satin, with a square yoke front and back of jet and heliotrope beads intermixed with large cabochons in jet. Another description of an evening gown at Bennetts of Sloane Street, says that, 'the perfectly fitting bodice of rich salmon pink satin, covered with thick gold tinsel gauze' is embroidered with a wheel-shaped pattern in tiny green, gold and brown iridescent beads. During the last part of the nineteenth century spangles on many garments and on net and on ribbon were mentioned. It was hinted that the use of spangles on lace led one to believe that the garment was a last year's model trying to look fashionably new.

Towards the end of the century bead embroidery became extremely popular, particularly in the elaboration of the decoration on bodices with the gored skirts left plain. Applied pattern also returned, face cloth with non-fraying edges being a popular fabric for this type of work, or inlay with the top fabric cut away in a design to show another colour beneath. Cording on the Cornely machine, in imitation of braids and also real braids were seen on day clothes.

The influence of peasant crafts was prevalent at the end of the century, due partly to greater travel facilities and to a better appreciation of foreign textiles. The Hazlemere Peasant Industries under the direction of Godfrey Blount in 1896 produced appliqué hangings in hand-woven, vegetable-dyed fabrics. The designs contained flat areas of colour devoid of shading, with shapes edged in satin stitch and sometimes with gold or silver threads. The Tree of Life was a favourite subject at this time, artists interpreting it in different ways. **M H Baillie Scott**, an architect, designed a great deal of embroidery, often for appliqué, with satin stitch and metal threads, using different colours and textures together, an innovation at this time. His work was well planned and he was probably one of the foremost designers of embroidery at the end of the century. (Page 57.)

1 1851 Berlin woolwork. 'The Last Supper.' A copy of Leonardo da Vinci's masterpiece. Signed 'Mrs J. Morris fecit 1851'. *Bethnal Green Museum, London*

2 Above: Early 1850s – Berlin woolwork. Small panel 13½ in. × 6⅛ in. (34 cm × 15 cm) on a fine canvas of 20 threads to the square inch. The panel is worked in silks and fine wools in tent stitch. The background is a reddish brown, the arch is in shades of reds, pinks and yellows, decorated with white spots. The columns are in tan wools and goldish silks. The base of the architecture is orange and cream with a pattern in reds and brownish red. The flowers are in reds, pinks and blues with cream. The leaves are in brown/greens with bottle green and lighter greens. The leaves at the base are in reds with green turnovers

3 Right: Early 1850s – Berlin woolwork. 'Arum lilies'. A hand-painted design on a printed squared paper. The design was copied from the coloured printed chart, although by 1851 designs were often printed directly onto the canvas

4 Left: Mid 1850s – Berlin woolwork. 17 in.(43 cm) long, on Penelope cotton canvas of 4 in. (10 cm) width, with the worked area of threads manipulated to give a single thread canvas. The daisies are in creams and pinks, the leaves in yellow greens, darker brownish greens with some leaves red, shading to ochre. Very fine wools are used for the embroidery in tent stitch. The work could have been for a dress accessory as the design is complete.

5 Above: Probably late 1850s or early 1860s – Berlin woolwork. Detail 12 in. (30.5 cm) long of part of a panel on Penelope canvas, worked in coarse wools. The background is black, the central panel dark red; orange geometric spirals are outlined in creamy yellow wool. In the middle of the panel a scarlet flower is outlined in thick cream silk and the centre is black. The half lower and upper central panels are green with mauve shapes outlined in cream silk as are the red leaves below and above the spirals, with smaller fawn leaves enclosed. Possibley for upholstery

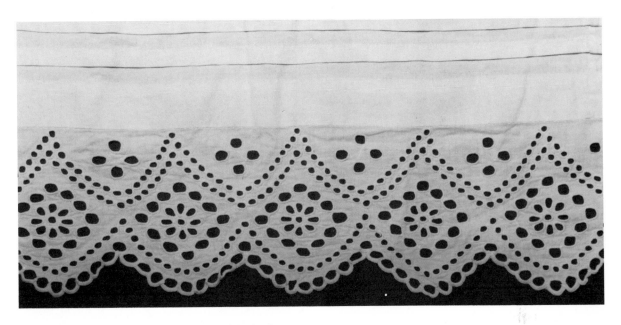

6 Late 1850s. A hand-embroidered broderie anglaise border on a petticoat. The petticoat is made entirely by hand in fine cotton; the embroidery is completely irregular on the back with no throwovers and all the threads are fastened off in different places. In machine-stitched broderie anglaise throwovers are regular in distribution

7 1861 George Street altar frontal. Frontal and superfrontal in St James-the-Less Church Westminster, London. Worked by the Ladies' Ecclesiastical Society or by the firm of Jones and Willis. The background is red velvet, with cream silk appliqué and canvas, silver and silver gilt threads, and cream cord, with embroidery in floss silks in cream, green, red, blue and peach. Laid work and couching with metal spangles decorate the frontal. According to the Victoria and Albert Museum's *Catalogue of Victorian Church Embroidery*, 1971, George Street used appliqué, floral motifs and monograms or crosses in many of his designs. *Victoria and Albert Museum, London*

8 1867 – W C Bangwyn. Banner of white silk, embroidered in coloured silks and gold threads. The lettering reads *Adoremus in aeternum sanctissimum sacramentum.* 59 in. × 39½ in. (150 × 100 cm). *Victoria and Albert Museum, London*

9 Below: 1875 – Edward Burne Jones and William Morris. A panel worked by the Royal School of Art Needlework in outline stitches in various shades of brown silk. *Victoria and Albert Museum, London*

10 Right: 1876 – William Morris. Coverlet of blue linen, embroidered in coloured silks by Catherine Holiday. The design is repetitive and consists of sunflowers and large leaves. *Victoria and Albert Museum, London*

11 Left, above: 1879 – Phoebe Traquair. A table cover worked in crewel wools, silk and gold threads. Flowers are in pinks and mauves with stamens in couched gold. The cactus stems are in green and brown silk and wool with spines in fly stitch. *Victoria and Albert Museum, London*

12 Left, below: 1886 – Altar frontal for St Mary's Convent, Wantage. Commenced in the 1870s, completed on Ascension Day 1886. A communal effort with different parts worked by different people in honour of St Mary Magdalene. The frontal was started by Sister Agnes who worked the figures of Our Lady and St Anna. Our Lady has a dark blue brocade garment with couched lines over it. St Joseph was worked by Miss Gillett or Sister Agnes; the boy with the doves by Sister Alice Margaret; Simeon and the Holy Child by Mrs H M Barker. All the features were worked by Sister Celia who made a speciality of these in embroidery. The background behind the figures is gold. The draperies are multi-coloured in long and short stitch. Gold haloes are couched in various colours and gold and black braids divide the panels. The buildings have gold domes and blue windows, and the columns are in twisted patterns of red and gold. The panels within the columns are dark grey-green with multi-coloured flowers; the side panels are of sage green brocade, with gold, padded pots and silk and gold leaves in long and short stitch and couching

13 Right: 1889 – Banner for St Mary's Convent, Wantage. The banner is worked on a coarse linen, with a laid work background of cream silk at the top, red at the bottom. The left-hand figure wears a cream vestment. The right-hand figure wears a bluish green cloak. Seed pearls and metal threads decorate the garments. The pot is in dark blue with couching and long and short stitches. The lettering is in yellow silk. The top band is multi-coloured, the architecture is in dark gold. Stitches are mainly long and short, couching, laid work, with a number of coloured silks used for the details. A new fringe was applied in 1900

14 Left: Late nineteenth century –
Walter Crane. A panel, 26 in. × 30 in.
(66 cm × 76 cm), worked entirely in silk
threads that cover the background. All
the shapes are outlined in brown silk
while the background is in a creamy
fawn with various details outlined in
brown. The standing Chinaman wears an
indigo-coloured coat with a robe in
fawn, patterned with turquoise spots
surrounded by cream. The lower robe is
blue and cream, and cream drapery
flows across the two figures. The
woman's garment is red with a fawnish
gold dress, and this colour is also used
for the turned-up hat brim. The seated
figure is in a red and orange streaked
garment, with a striped pattern in gold
and bright blue. Other details are in
pale greys and creams. The flesh is
natural in colour, the Chinaman's
yellowish. *Victoria and Albert Museum,
London*

15 Right: Late nineteenth century. A
child's dress of white cotton broderie
anglaise, entirely stitched by machine

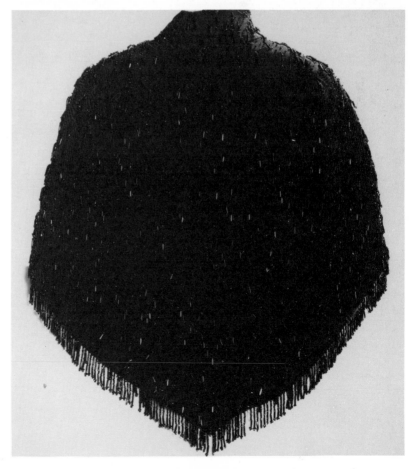

16 Right: Late nineteenth century,
probably 1880s. A short cape in black
corded silk, with French jet beads which
are free hanging. Small beads are also
scattered over the surface and these give
a shimmering appearance when the
wearer moves

17 Right: Twentieth-century Ruskin work. A pincushion by Oenone Cave, on evenweave linen in the manner of the Ruskin work of the late nineteenth century. Needleweaving, buttonhole, bullion knots and pulled work are combined in one piece of embroidery

18 Below: The Leek Embroidery Society. Part of a border, called by Rachel K Shuttleworth 'The Indian Style', worked on tussah silk over a printed pattern in reddish brown. Floss silks and gold threads are used for the embroidery in long and short stitch and couching. The work is probably for a mantlepiece border and in Rachel's own words, described as 'very handsome'. The colours are four different greens, three browns, three blues and three reds. The design repeats every $4\frac{3}{8}$ in. (11.2 cm). The size of the piece is $15\frac{7}{8}$ in. $\times 5\frac{3}{4}$ in. (40.3 cm $\times$ 14.7 cm). The pattern was printed by the firm of Thomas Wardle. *Loaned by Gawthorpe Hall*

The end of the nineteenth century

Many of the enterprises at the end of the century were the inspiration behind the embroidery of the early nineteen hundreds. Most schools of art included embroidery in their curricula, and new schools were being opened while those long established were changing their images. In 1896 the Central School of Arts and Crafts was opened. This was formerly the old government School of Design, established in 1837 in Somerset House. In 1897 the Royal College of Art took the place of the National Art Training School in South Kensington. Embroidery was later introduced into both of these institutions.

Technical instruction in crafts and in design was given, with the aim of linking up with manufacture where possible. Embroidery remained an educational study except in areas where there was textile manufacture and some connection with the subject in industry. Craft and drawing classes were held in the schools, the work of the embroiderer being of a practical nature, for dress or the adornment of household articles and for ecclesiastical vestments and furnishings.

The Arts and Crafts Movement flourished; artists of note including painters, designers and architects, continued to design for embroidery. Some artists, such as M H Scott, designed and executed their own work. In other cases the embroidery was carried out by their wives and friends.

Fisherton-de-la-Mer Industries

In the 1890s some individuals of note were branching out in different directions. Among these was **Josephine Newall** who founded the Fisherton-de-la-Mer Industries, which flourished under her guidance for 30 years. This enterprise was started as a means of providing occupation for disabled men and women and to give them a new and absorbing interest to occupy their minds. The idea was developed from Josephine Newall's love of old two-sided Italian cross-stitch embroideries in red silk on linen, and from Italian whitework of the seventeenth and eighteenth centuries. She studied old Italian books and collected Italian and English linen work of these centuries, adapting the designs for her own use. The cottage industry grew from one pupil, who started in 1890 or 1892. Materials with diagrams and instructions were often sent by post to the workers, who returned the finished embroidery for criticism. The work was rarely unpicked, thus encouraging sound craftsmanship. Linen stitches were the basis of much of the embroidery (pages 34, 35, 73). Those skilled enough were allowed to choose their own stitches, the really advanced workers planning their own designs to fit in with the instructions issued on the type and size of the work. When there was difficulty in obtaining the hand-spun and hand-woven linens, loosely woven Russian linens and Chinese linens were used. Finishings such as lace and tassels were selected with great care. The standard of workmanship became excellent and the embroidery was widely exhibited. Embroideries exhibited in San Francisco during the First World War led to many orders from the United States.

Josephine Newall said that embroidery could not be accomplished without industry as well as patience and that different designs were necessary for the different qualities of materials, the best generally being the simplest.

Another embroiderer, **Mary Newill** was a versatile artist by all accounts who carried out book illustration and stained glass as well as specialising in embroidery. She was well-known for her large pictorial hangings which contained a great deal of stitchery, using crewel wools or sometimes appliqué with stitchery She exhibited widely, gaining several prizes. Her work was influenced by Edward Burne-Jones whom she admired. She was a member of the Arts and Crafts Exhibition Society, also of the Bromsgrove Guild of Handicrafts, and in her teaching developed what became known as the Birmingham method of embroidery. This was the working of flowers and other subjects straight onto the material without preliminary drawing. She became well known for her success with the work done by students.

Art Nouveau in Scotland

In Scotland Charles Rennie Mackintosh, an architect and teacher, evolved a strong personal style of Art Nouveau, with two-dimensional linear elegance in design. This achieved an international reputation. With an architectural bias, his imaginatively drawn plants with tenuous stems supported stylised flowers, interlaced in intricate patterns. The results were so distinctive as to warrant the title of 'The Glasgow School of Art Scottish Style Art Nouveau'. Between 1897 and 1904 Mackintosh designed the Glasgow School of Art and four tea-rooms; the last one, the Willow Tea Room, became the most famous. His wife, Margaret Macdonald, an artist and embroiderer (page 61), designed the interior of this building. Mackintosh's style pervaded the Glasgow School of Art which produced excellent embroidery during the nineties, much ahead of that in England, where art needlework still flourished and the copying of historic examples persisted.

The Glasgow School of Art

The advanced teaching in the Glasgow School of Art was due to **Jessie Rowat**, the daughter of a shawl manufacturer. She had travelled widely with her parents, collecting old embroideries, many from the Balkan States. She became a student in Glasgow where she was influenced by the artists there, marrying the head of the School, Frank Newbery. In 1894 she taught embroidery, at first modifying the ideas of William Morris, but soon evolving her own style. She believed in good drawing, original design in which she was keenly interested, and in sound technique as long as this did not dominate the idea. Her aim was simplicity of approach but using good quality materials, often from Liberty, with stitchery worked in silk threads, or in crewel wools (pages 38, 47, 48, 49, 53). In her teaching she introduced appliqué of simple shapes with designs often composed mainly of lettering and needleweaving. She embroidered panels in silks on linen. Ann Macbeth, formerly one of her students, later her assistant, was influenced by her style. As well as designing clothes for children she taught students to embroider simple decoration on garments. She disliked the dark colours then in fashion, and so made individual colour schemes, particularly in the decoration of dress, where her interest in the peasant arts was put to good use with embroidery based on Balkan and Russian styles. Jessie Newbery became well known for her particular outlook on costume. She and two of her friends, Margaret and Frances Macdonald, designed their own clothes, which were distinctive. These were often embroidered, loose garments, associated with the styles of the aesthetic movement in dress. The sisters were both good artists and Frances, who married Herbert McNair, an architect, assisted Ann Macbeth from 1909 to 1911.

The work started by Jessie Newbery, with her interest in lettering, appliqué and the use of the human figure was continued by **Ann Macbeth**, who had entered the school originally to study life drawing and anatomy. She became fascinated by embroidery when she assisted Jessie Newbery in her classes, and was herself an inspiring teacher. She started with simple techniques using ordinary materials, such as flannel and calico, making students produce their own designs by building up stitch patterns; she organised children's classes and had a great influence on embroidery in Scotland, particularly in the west. Her own work showed an individual style and in 1902 she exhibited with Jessie Newbery in Turin. She produced large and small figurative hangings completely stitched, or in appliqué and stitching. She embroidered domestic articles and undertook commissions for secular and ecclesiastical work; she also designed for Liberty's, for Knox's Linen Thread Company and for Donald Brothers, Dundee. In an article written for *The Studio* magazine in 1903 Ann Macbeth was praised for her practical outlook on the adornment of dress and for her use of good quality but ordinary materials, of sound colour – which were improved with embroidery. Her ambition was to embroider backgrounds until she was a competent draughtswoman. She was a hard and prolific worker and embroidered household linens, dress, book covers and banners, among other things, and exhibited in London and in Glasgow. In 1911 she collaborated with Margaret Swanson on a book *Educational Needlecraft* which had an entirely new approach to the subject, giving a progressive course for schools in plain sewing and in embroidery. In the opening words on the scheme the authors say: 'One method of instruction lies through that ancient and cheap tool – the needle – which gives the form of stitchery, and through material, which gives the colour which becomes one by means of art.' They also mention 'the necessity for freedom in experimental work'. (Pages 54, 55.)

This book had great impact on the teaching of needlework and a scheme was devised to send examples described in the book in parcels to schools both in Great Britain and abroad. The idea grew, and was most successful.

Ann Macbeth organised summer schools and courses and took as students those with domestic science diplomas, who were allowed to attend the school for advanced study of needlework and embroidery.

When Jessie Newbery retired in 1908, Ann Macbeth took over the embroidery department. Barbara Morris in her book *Victorian Embroidery* says 'an entirely new approach to embroidery was evolved at the Glasgow School of Art, an approach that was to lay the foundation for the embroidery of our own time, particularly in the educational field . . . the influence was felt even in the 1920s and the basic principles laid down for the teaching of embroidery are by and large the same as those in force today'. Jessie Newbery and Ann Macbeth taught design and decorative art to classes in 1904. Continuation classes were held for evening students and preparatory classes in drawing for those wishing to follow a training at the School of Art when they left school, the Glasgow School Board being ahead of English art education. A report on the classes for teachers in art needlework in 1905, by H M Inspector Frank Young, for prospective teachers, says:

'For the first time special classes in Art Needlework were instituted this session; seldom has any art class been so fully successful in all respects. The satchels of needlework, the portfolios of drawings and studies and the final inspection exercises were without exception highly praiseworthy . . . students who have passed through this course have proved their ability in drawing, design and needlework and they should now be able to take the intelligent direction of similar work as required by the Scotch Education dept.'

A Saturday class was started in 1904 with Ann Macbeth as instructor, and a report of 1907–8 says that the teachers' Saturday classes produced some excellent results. It also says that embroidery was designed on paper and carried out on appropriate materials '. . . beautiful work is being carried out by the ladies in the embroidery class'. In the prospectus for 1906–7 an account of the Glasgow School of Art says that it was the central institution for higher art education for Glasgow and the west of Scotland in 1901, with no connection with the English Board of Education. The syllabus for design and decoration was stiff. Students had to pass a preparatory course before entering the design room. Embroidery was part of the advanced course, where students worked out programmes of various subjects such as a mantelpiece border, embroidered in colours of their own choice. The technical art studies provided for needlework. In 1910 the day school diploma course consisted of elementary and advanced study. The elementary section included stitching, constructional decoration and instruction in simple geometric floral design; for the advanced section life drawing and figure composition were necessary as a preliminary.

There was a two-year certificate course in needlework and embroidery too, both of these courses requiring drawing, design and practical application. (See *Embroidery*, Vol 24, No. 4 – Margaret Swain.) Frank Newbery suggested that all female students should study embroidery.

A number of banners were produced for the British Association for the Advancement of Science, some of which were embroidered (page 53). A banner dated 1901 was double-sided, one of these being worked by Jessie Newbery, the other by Ann Macbeth. This banner commemorated Professor Rucker. Each of the embroiderers signed their work.

Artists in England

In England several artists prominent in the Arts and Crafts Movement were designing for textiles and writing on the techniques of embroidery, as well as approaches to design. Among these was **Lewis F Day**, an industrial artist who produced many designs for textiles and embroidery (page 35). In opposition to the ideas of William Morris, he believed in the future of the machine, suggesting that because of it, styles in decoration might be changed. He wrote a number of books including *Nature and Ornament* in 1896, and others on pattern, lettering and stained glass. In 1900 he wrote *Art and Needlework*, in which he said: 'Embroidery is often thought of as an idle accomplishment. It is more than that. At the very least it is a handicraft; at the best an art'. He believed too in the division of labour between the artist who designed the embroidery and the worker who carried it out. He thought that the ideal, in which the idea was designed and executed by one person, was mainly impossible: either the good design would be spoilt in the working for want of executive skill on the part of the designer, or good workmanship would be spent on poor design.

Walter Crane, who followed Morris's tradition, believed in the hand-made crafts as the true root and basis of all art' (first catalogue of the Arts and Crafts Exhibition Society, 1888). He wrote the preface to the first edition of *Embroidery or the Craft of the Needle*, 1899, by W Paulson Townsend, in which he said: 'If taste can be said to be of more importance in one art than another it is certainly all important in needlework. It enters in every stage – in planning appropriate design, in change of scale, in choice of materials, and above all, of colour'.

Summary 1851–1900

Prominent people

Mrs Beeton

George Frederick Bodley, architect and designer of ecclesiastical vestments

George Street, architect, designer of ecclesiastical furnishings

William Morris, architect, painter, designer, weaver, embroiderer, writer

W Curtis Brangwyn, architect, designer of ecclesiastical embroidery

Lady Marian Alford, authoress, Vice President Royal School of Art Needlework

Phoebe Traquair

Mary Newill

Walter Crane

Selwyn Image

Lewis F Day

Jessie Newbery

Josephine Newall

Charles Rennie Mackintosh

Margaret Macdonald

M H Baillie Scott

May Morris

Ann Macbeth

Margaret Swanson

Societies, schools exhibitions	**1854**	The Ladies' Ecclesiastical Embroidery Society
	1857	National Art Training School
	1862	The Great International Exhibition
	1863	Link up between the Ladies' Ecclesiastical Embroidery Society and the Wantage Church Needlework Association
	1872	Royal School of Art Needlework
	1875	Ladies' Work Society – others were formed in various cities in Britain
	1876	Philadelphia Centennial Exhibition
	1879	Leek Embroidery Society
	1880	Decorative Needlework Society
	1882	The Century Guild
	1883	Home Arts and Industries Association
	1884	The Art Workers' Guild
	1888	First exhibition – Arts and Crafts Exhibition Society
	1890	Second exhibition – Arts and Crafts Exhibition Society
	1894	First competition held by the Worshipful Company of Broderers
	1896	Exhibition, Arts and Crafts Exhibition Society
	1896	The Central School of Arts and Crafts opened
	1897	The Royal College of Art opened

Commercial enterprises	**1861**	Morris, Marshall and Faulkner Watts and Co (ecclesiastical furnishers) now in Tufton Street, Westminster
	1874	William Briggs – Manchester
	1875	Arthur Liberty – London
	1879	Thomas Wardle – Leek
	1888	Arthur Lee – Warrington and Birkenhead
	1890s	Fisherton-de-la-Mer Industries Hazlemere Peasant Industries

Main types of embroidery	**1850 –70**	Berlin woolwork – most popular Broderie anglaise – superseded Ayrshire work Patchwork continued throughout nineteenth century Quilting continued throughout nineteenth century
	1851	Coggershall lace Art needlework – surface stitching often in silk threads
	1880s	Smocking on women's and children's clothes
	1880s	Whitework – cut work, mainly richelieu, broderie anglais, drawn threadwork
	1880s	Ruskin lace Filet net embroidery Ecclesiastical embroidery – banners, frontals Influence of Japanese work
	1895	Influence of Art Nouveau Cross-stich on fabric printed for the purpose French canvas embroidery – on single thread

Bead embroidery
Machine embroidery in the trade

Magazines and books

(a)

(b)

19 Late nineteenth century or early twentieth century. Josephine Newall – Fisherton-de-la-Mer Industries. Two mats worked in natural linen thread on natural linen, each 4¼ in. (10.7 cm) square. (a) The centre is in needlemade lace in knotted buttonhole, needleweaving and bars with picots. The border is in eyelet and satin stitches with four-sided stitch. Buttonhole loops decorate the edges of the mat. (b) The centre is in needlemade lace in knotted buttonhole and buttonhole bars with picots. The border is in pulled work and four-sided stitch. The edges are decorated with buttonhole loops and triangles of knotted buttonhole. *Loaned by Mrs Judd*

20 Late nineteenth century or early twentieth century. Josephine Newall – Fisherton-de-la-Mer Industries. Part of a border on a runner, worked on natural linen in linen thread. The main border is in satin stitch with pulled thread worked to give diagonal stripes. The smaller borders are in satin stitch with algerian eye stitch and enclosed borders in needleweaving giving a cross-like structure. Hem stitching divides each border. *Loaned by Mrs Judd*

21 1896 – Lewis F Day. A panel, 35 in. × 18 in. (88 cm × 45.7 cm) for a firescreen worked in floss silks by his wife. *Victoria and Albert Museum, London*

22 Left: Approximately 1895. An evening gown of cream satin, machine-made lace and silk gauze, with embroidery, worked in satin stitch on the Irish machine, applied separately. The embroidery is heavily padded and multi-coloured. Fine twisted threads are used in pinks, cream, dark plum, blues, greens and reds. A fine metal braid edges the skirt. *Victoria and Albert Museum, London*

23 Above: Late nineteenth century. Detail of a border on a red velvet evening coat. Embroidered on the Cornely machine in yellows and reds, with iridescent beads in pearly mauves, yellowish reds and yellows with a greenish tinge. The coat is lavishly embroidered and theatrical in style. The border is approximately 6 in. (15 cm) deep. *Loaned to the Embroiderers' Guild by Mrs Lauder*

24 Right: Late nineteenth century. A corner of a tablecloth in white linen, showing a number of techniques. The wide border is composed of needlewoven bars connected to woven braid which is joined again with spiders' webs to form tree-like forms. A square of machine-made filet net is darned to make a pattern of a vase of flowers and leaves in the corner. Strips of linen are joined with spiders' webs sewn to the woven braid edges. Broderie anglaise is worked down the centre of the 48 in. (122 cm) long linen strips. The cloth is 72 in. (183 cm) square with the centre composed of a filet net square, surrounded by a border of filet net, each darned with abstract semi-geometrical shapes. Surrounding this central area are alternating 7 in. (17.7 cm) squares of filet net, each darned with a symmetrical pattern of flowers and leaves, alternating with 7 in. × 4 in. (17.7 cm × 10 cm) strips of linen worked in broderie anglaise

25 1897 – Jessie Newbery. Detail of a mantle border, designed by Jessie Newbery and worked by Edith Rowat, her mother. The background is natural linen worked in a repetitive pattern in crewel wools, in green, dull turquoise, blue, pinks and purple. Stitches include long and short, stem, satin, french knots and straight stitches. The border is in drawn thread work. 26 in. × 99½ in. (66 cm × 259.8 cm). Shown in the 1916 Glasgow Exhibition. *In the collection of the Glasgow School of Art*

The first decade of the twentieth century

A new era began in the twentieth century, with the development of technical and scientific knowledge, social changes, and a widening appreciation of the arts and artists. Many hitherto sound beliefs and principles were questioned. There was a great gulf at the beginning of the century between the wealthy and the poverty stricken workers, who suffered appalling housing conditions and inadequate wages. But elementary education improved and the suffragette movement came into being.

Interest in embroidery

It is evident from the activities of this decade that crafts, including embroidery, were taken seriously and that among professional designers and teachers there was a great deal of talent and enormous interest. Embroiderers, however, were a minority group within the art world, tending to be ignored by those who practised 'fine art'. The advocates of original design were few, although there were many technically skilled artists who could copy superbly.

The awareness that there was a lack of design in manufactured goods persisted at the beginning of the century. It was realised that there was a great need for industrial designers and for teachers who could overcome the penchant for the copying of the traditions of the past.

Schools of art

The schools of art were now flourishing and were aiming to train artists and craftsmen to fulfil the need for trained designers. Crafts were popular and although embroidery was based on tradition, there were signs of change, encouraged by artists such as Walter Crane, Lewis F Day and M H Baillie Scott (pages 12, 16, 18). The Central School of Arts and Crafts, the Royal College of Art and other art institutions training teachers and designers also began to have some effect in the schools and in industry.

Embroidery in the Scottish schools was in advance of that in English schools which continued to work in the art needlework tradition until after the First World War. The copying of old embroideries and historic styles was prevalent and transfers were popular among amateur embroiderers. Much work in schools was still historically orientated, although original design was given more thought and space filling, employing plant forms in the style of William Morris, continued into the 1920s in the schools of art, sometimes being translated into embroidery in silk or crewel wools on linen.

According to an article written early in the century, the Birmingham Central School of Arts and Crafts was training students in 'artistic crafts' practised in the city. Embroidery was one of these, taught by practising craftsmen. Compared with the average trade standards, the artistic level was high. It was considered also that it was important to train the amateur student, who was a potential buyer. It was assumed in the teaching that the manipulation of materials was a natural way in which design would grow.

Art needlework requisites were advertised in many women's magazines. Art stitchery transfers were printed for embroidery on silk or linen, but combining different threads and fabrics and using a variety of techniques in one piece of work remained taboo for some time to come. The tendency to concentrate on floral design, which was always popular, gave way to an interest in geometric patterns although sometimes the two were combined. Peasant art was a basis of much of the embroidery at this time.

The pictorial sampler was fashionable during the early part of the century. Sometimes it was in the form of a pictorial record, containing a variety of techniques. Darning, blackwork patterns, pulled work and surface stitchery were intermingled as in Doris Taylor's 'Fox and Grapes' (page 87) and 'The Blue Bird' (page 86). Other samplers could be records of stitches and techniques, for example one by Mildred Lockyer which represented as many stitches and methods of working as possible. The variety of fringes, cords, tassels, and embroidered buttons made for interesting finishings (page 117).

Dress

Hardangar work decorated dress as did embroidery based on the work seen on peasant costume. Lace began to take the place of embroidery during the first decade of the twentieth century, as Nottingham was producing quantities of machine-made lace which was comparatively cheap. An article from a magazine published in November 1904 describes an evening gown with a bolero embroidered in green and gold silk, with real silver thread, in a raised design of roses. Boleros were fashionable, in many different fabrics, velvet ones embroidered in gold and silver thread being particularly popular. Handbags were beaded, made of kid and embroidered in metal threads. Belts stitched in a variety of ways were also fashionable. Lavish use of metal thread embroidery was seen on leather and cloth, on hats and accessories. The meandering stems and floral devices at this time still showed the influence of the Art Nouveau style.

Exhibitions

Exhibitions created great interest in the late nineteenth century, including those of major societies such as the Arts and Crafts Exhibition Society in England, which, like the local societies, accepted embroidery. These exhibitions continued in popularity, embroidery and other crafts sometimes being shown together, sometimes separately. In 1901 an inspiring show of samplers at the Fine Arts Society premises led to the publication of a book on *Samplers and Tapestries* by Marius Huish. At this time too an exhibition in Glasgow created enormous enthusiasm for the new approach to embroidery, but this had little effect on English work until later.

For some time magazines had been encouraging interest in the crafts by running competitions in embroidery. Among the better magazines was *The Studio* which promoted competitions for embroidery and lace; from the illustrations it seems that lively, well designed articles in an Art Nouveau style were prevalent. They included collars, belts and other dress accessories, cushion covers and household embroideries (pages 48, 49, 54). The magazine advertised art needlework or embroidery classes among the subjects available in the schools of art. Reviews of current exhibitions in Great Britain and abroad were given, often referring to embroidery. In reviewing an exhibition in Turin in 1902 the magazine mentioned the arts and crafts section as containing some superb, very large embroidered panels, pictorial in content worked very finely in silks. These were the embroideries submitted from Great Britain by Jessie Newbery and Ann Macbeth.

Liverpool Cathedral embroideries

G F Bodley was asked to design frontals for Liverpool Cathedral, which had from 1902 to 1932 a Cathedral Embroidery Association. This Association worked ten of the fourteen frontals in the Cathedral, five for the Lady Chapel being used first in 1910. They also worked five for the high altar. George Bodley was impressed by the skill of the Association, as in 1903 he had suggested that figurative work was beyond them. In 1904 he was asked to design frontals, but the Association had not been consulted. However, he submitted three designs in 1905 for the Lady Chapel, in white, green and red; the green one was worked by Miss Margaret and Miss Muriel Comber. The white festal frontal was in couched gold and raised work in coloured silks. All the embroideries had to be approved by George Bodley's firm of Watts and Company. In 1906 he showed to the authorities a design containing four angels, which was worked by the Association, using some fabrics specially dyed; this was finished by 1910.

When George Bodley died in 1907 Cecil G Hare became the designer and adviser to the Embroidery Association. He designed the Passiontide frontal, commenced in 1910.

Coronation robes and costume

In 1902 lavish embroidery in gold and silver threads was seen at the coronation of Edward VII, both in the military and civil costume. The cloth of gold vestments worn by the King were embroidered by the Royal School of Art Needlework on gold tissue, the design including, besides the emblems of the British Empire, crowns, eagles, olive branches and passion flowers. Queen Alexandra's robe of purple velvet was embroidered by the Ladies' Work Society, again containing symbols of the British Empire depicted as a rose tree, with a Saxon crown from which sprang shamrocks and thistles, with fleur-de-lis at the roots. Crowns were scattered over the robe; her dress was in gold tissue, overlaid with white net, embroidered with gold spangles and gold and silver floral sprays and was made in Paris (page 56).

Descriptions of the gowns worn by guests suggest that embroidery was profusely used in their decoration. One worn by a Miss M J H Buckland was of cream twilled silk and white cotton, with a leaf pattern almost covering it, worked in gold-coloured untwisted silk in chain stitch. The suggestion by the London Museum is that it could be of Indian origin, although the label inside is Harris and Toms, Manchester Square (*Coronation Costume 1685–1953*).

Embroidery was obviously of general interest to both the professional and amateur artist as current events in schools of art were described in detail in the arts and crafts magazines. One description in 1903 praised the Newark School of Art for an excellent show of embroideries, the Headmaster being congratulated on obtaining permission to hold embroidery classes, which were taught by Miss E H Tann, trained at the Royal School of Art Needlework. She and Marguerite Randall received their teaching diplomas in December 1902 at the ceremony attended by such well-known people as Allan Cole, Arthur Liberty and George Frampton RA, the director of the evening classes. The technical evening classes and the training courses for professional workers and teachers had started six years previously at the Royal School of Art Needlework.

Marguerite Randall, after receiving her teaching diploma, studied lacemaking in Bruges and Buckinghamshire. She also studied figurative embroidery. For a time she taught in South Africa but her voice was affected by the altitude. She returned home, taught part-time at the Royal School of Art Needlework, becoming the Mistress of the training school from 1912 until 1951. She was keen on both secular and ecclesiastical embroidery, had excellent technique in all aspects of the craft and was knowledgeable about the history of the craft. Many of her holidays were spent in Belgium and France, gathering new ideas and continuing to study figure work.

M H Baillie Scott wrote an article in *The Studio* magazine in 1903 entitled 'Some experiments in embroidery', in which he suggested a new approach, whose aim was not to vie with other arts such as painting in producing realistic shading.

In February 1903 the Arts and Crafts Exhibition Society held its seventh show at the New Gallery. It was remarked that 'the movement of 1888 continues to show abundant signs of life and vigour . . . the effect of its influence at home and abroad is no less remarkable'. A great deal of embroidery was submitted, the critic quoting May Morris who, writing on line embroidery had said – 'needlework should be irresponsible, gay, a little absurd sometimes, but very personal'. All of these qualities, apparently, were present in work in the exhibition.

The human figure in embroidery

The human figure was popular in design at the beginning of the century, worked entirely in stitchery or with stitchery and appliqué, lettering sometimes being incorporated into the scheme. Allegorical subjects were favourites; the concept was romantic, even sentimental, and purely pictorial. At the exhibition of 1903 Phoebe Traquair presented one of her most important works, a four-fold screen, started in 1895 (page 51). These panels took seven years to complete. Walter Crane showed a portière embroidered by his wife, while Grace Christie submitted doilies. Delicate colours such as pale rose, grey green, silver and white were much in evidence at the exhibition.

Grace Christie was influential in raising standards during the early twentieth century. She was well-known for her embroideries at the beginning of the century; studying originally as a painter, she had no formal training in the subject and did not teach before becoming the first instructor of embroidery at the Royal College of Art, from 1909 to 1921. Her book *Embroidery and Tapestry Weaving*, published in 1906, contained an excellent chapter on design and ways in which to begin to make a pattern. She was inspired by the exhibition of samplers in 1901, finding the show most stimulating. Her book was written as a result. Through her interest in embroidery, Grace Christie possessed a thorough knowledge of its history and its many techniques, her main concern being with traditional work and fine craftsmanship. She had a passion for the country, flowers in particular, working floral designs in fine silks on linen, but using very few varieties of stitch. Sometimes she introduced lettering. She was interested in what stitches could do, in their textures and the richness of surface obtainable. Frequently she worked in monotones, white on white or cream on white, where the colour would not override the stitchery and the raised surfaces of some of the more intricate techniques. Grace Christie was keen to use stitches worked flatly in solid colours, in contrast to the current trend for shading in long and short stitches which imitated painting. She insisted that her students should use clear colours with stitches worked quite flat to give texture. She was from all accounts a martinet, who forbade students to carry on with work outside her classes; those who did had to unpick all that they had done unsupervised. Her idea was that embroidery should be for posterity, therefore it must be as good as possible in every aspect. She disagreed with Lewis F Day when he said '. . . a slight acquaintance with drawing and design is sufficient'. She believed that '. . . drawing ability is necessary to enable the worker to set down her ideas upon paper. For much simple and pretty work, however, a slight acquaintance with drawing and design is sufficient and anyone who can master the requisite stitches can also acquire some knowledge of these two subjects'. (Page 86 and colour plate 7.)

In the Victoria and Albert Museum Library there is a volume of six magazines edited by Grace Christie in 1909. These were published by Pearsall and Company at sixpence per copy. Each magazine contained articles on techniques, on designing with flowers and on dress accessories with excellent diagrams and photographs.

In 1914 Grace Christie edited a magazine *Needle and Thread* which was discontinued with the advent of war. She was an examiner in embroidery for the City and Guilds of London Institute from 1923 to 1927 and possibly earlier, as she examined in 1919. Her book *Samplers and Stitches* was published in 1920, in which she said: 'By the aid of stitches a monotonous surface can be transformed at will into a rich and varied one'. Students lived with her in her home while working a number of the samples for the book. Her greatest work was a detailed study of *Opus Anglicanum* embroidery, *English Medieval Embroidery*, published in 1938. This was inspired by the Exhibition of English Embroidery held in 1905 at the Burlington Fine Arts Club. For this book she spent many holidays abroad, obtaining photographs of ecclesiastical embroideries not available in England.

An example of a piece of work for the City and Guilds of London Institute examinations, worked probably in 1910 by **Katherine Powell**, shows meticulous technique with a strong pictorial style (pages 74, 75). With one hand she produced some excellent work. She took both the ordinary level and the advanced level examinations, one in 1908, the other in 1919 when she gained a silver medal. Her examiner was Grace Christie. For two pieces of work entered for the Board of

Education National Competition in 1911 she gained two bronze medals. These were for a child's quilted bonnet and embroidered collar and cuffs.

She taught art and needlework and was an excellent draughtswoman (Joan Edwards, *Embroidery*, Winter 1978).

The Worshipful Company of Broderers

The Worshipful Company of Broderers held a competitive exhibition in April 1903, their first having been in 1894. There were different categories of work and 21 prizes: (A) for figure embroidery only, sacred or secular; faces and hands to be embroidered (this was stipulated as they were sometimes painted); size not less than 12 in. × 54 in. (30.5 cm × 137 cm); (B) for embroidery, sacred or secular, done on a frame, shaded in silks, or in silks and gold; not less than 30 in. × 18 in. (76 cm × 45.7 cm); (C) for embroidery as applied to any articles of ornament or utility, appliqué work or hand work, silks or crewels, shaded or for the adaptation of the greatest variety of stitches. Design, colour and execution had to be by the exhibitor.

The exhibition took place at the new premises of the Royal School of Art Needlework. The promotors felt that if a little more stress had been laid on the design, the competition would have been productive of better results. In section (A) Mary Symonds received a prize of £5. In (B) Lewis F Day's design, worked by Mary Buckle, was awarded 15 guineas for work which was a glorious piece of colour and a perfect example of embroidery, while Ann Macbeth, according to the critic, appeared to have been overlooked by the judges as her work was excellent but not even mentioned.

In the same year the Board of Education's exhibition of the National Competitions of Schools of Art and Art Classes held their exhibition for the first time at the Victoria and Albert Museum's new galleries. The report on the embroidery by the examiners was that there was a greater number of better works than usual, but no individual work was of the excellence of the best submitted in 1902.

An ecclesiastical exhibition

In 1905 an important exhibition of early English ecclesiastical embroidery was held at Burlington House by the Burlington Fine Arts Club. A magnificent catalogue on *Opus Anglicanum*, entitled *English Embroidery*, was issued, well illustrated in colour and black and white, with an introduction by A F Kendrick, and detailed descriptions of each piece of work.

The Society of Certificated Embroideresses

In 1906, 16 past students of the Royal School of Art Needlework formed a society to keep up the standards of embroidery. This was the Society of Certificated Embroideresses, each member paying a subscription of two shillings and sixpence per year. Although at first the society accepted only those who had the two years' certificate of the School and a teacher's diploma, it was realised that a wider membership was desirable and on consultation with Alfred East ARA, George Frampton RA, Walter Crane, Lewis F Day and others, embroiderers were allowed membership if their work was of a sufficiently high standard. A portfolio of designs, passed by W Paulson Townsend, was kept for the use of members. In 1907 the Worshipful Company of Broderers became vice-patrons.

Embroidery for the home

In interior design a greater simplicity was noticeable, although every style seemed to be fashionable from the mediaeval to the Elizabethan, the Italian eighteenth century and the 'olde worlde' cottage style with oak beams. Embroidered cushions, curtains and table covers were popular and unframed wall hangings were becoming fashionable. In *The Studio Year Books* articles on different crafts appeared. One in *The Studio Year Book* for 1906 showed a table cover and hanging by Ann Macbeth, also cartoons for large panels, to be embroidered, designed by J N Dearle, the designer from the firm of William Morris and Co. The text is interesting and says '. . . embroidery is an art . . . which ought to be sumptuous and finely wrought . . . cheap embroidery is a contradiction in terms. Machine-made imitations of chain stitch . . . are unworthy to exist at all. . . . A brocaded silk should not be used for embroidery, some say . . . but too many mediaeval instances . . . contravene this canon . . . to condemn the practice'. A description of some of the works seen in exhibitions followed, saying that simple, applied shapes were popular, sewn down with buttonhole or couched with gold thread outlines, solid embroidery in darning, tent and satin stitch, worked quite flatly, avoided any shaded effects: 'the . . . effect depending mainly on beauty of drawing . . . chiefest of all . . . colour . . . which may be bright or even gay'. Vegetable dyes were advocated for subtlety, and to obtain richness of effect it was suggested that gold thread outlines sewn down with coloured silks would give the embroidery a sparkle. In *The Studio Year Book* of 1907, the writer of an article on embroidery said 'Embroidery is of the nature of an extra embellishment, and as such ought always to be rich and sumptuous, else it belies itself and is without justification. Silk stitchery or appliqué . . . may adorn the poorer material of linen or woollen cloth, but a silk web is not adequately enhanced by the addition of crewel or cotton threadwork.'

The Glasgow style

Ann Macbeth's work and that of her associates and students was criticised as having the stamp of the Glasgow School of Art which although 'novel and fantastic' in design, colour and execution was unmistakeable in style. This was a severe conventionalisation of form and strange blendings of subdued colours such as mauve, green, white and brown and greyish pinks used together.

Appliqué edged with satin stitch, chain-stitched flowers and the 'Glasgow' roses were recurring techniques and styles of the period as was drawn thread work combined with appliqué and surface embroidery (pages 54, 55, 61).

Modern embroidery in 1907

In *Needlecraft Monthly* for June 1907, an article says: 'Modern embroidery seems to be a follow on from the Victorian embroidery, in shading, or the embroidery is all traditional peasant in style. There is no original design, hardangar drawn thread combined with embroidery is a favourite'. Art needlework novelties advertised at Messrs William Whiteley suggest that . . . 'the pretty iris design is the favourite work of the season, for table covers, duchesse sets, all in unbleached linen with the design already painted, to be worked in silks'. Another comment is 'dresses in linen with embroidery and lace combined, are fashionable, but . . . there is hardly a Parisian gown for dressy occasions, which does not exhibit a mixture of gold and silver thread . . . so many of the waistcoats, vests and bodices this season are adorned with minute motifs in ribbon work'. Broderie anglaise parasols, medallions of silk stitchery on silk and satin parasols, were smart at this time, but the general complaint was that these were adaptations from 'old stuff'.

W Paulson Townsend edited the *Art Workers' Quarterly* which supplied designs for craftsmen who were unable to design for themselves, and in the second edition of his book in 1907 he says of embroidery '. . . there is little likelihood of its ever regaining sway and filling those serious . . . functions which were once the very essence of its being. Today it is treated more as a graceful diversion . . . although there is a serious attempt to reanimate the long neglected art of embroidery'. Although there was still an awareness of the need for design education, embroidery was now low on the list of serious art forms. At this time letters received by the *Needlecraft Monthly* magazine suggested that 'there was a real demand for a magazine devoted to needlecraft alone'. There were more and more women's magazines published but embroidery was a small feature in them, knitting, crochet, beauty, etc, taking up much of the space.

Advice on design given in books

A Book of Studies of Plant Form with some suggestions for their application to design by A E Lilley and W Midgley, published in 1907, remarked that there was a return to nature, especially floral forms, as opposed to obtaining inspiration for design from historic ornament. It was also noted that the 'function of ornament is to add interest to construction'.

In connection with the proliferation of women's magazines **Flora Klickmann** should be mentioned as a promoter of interest in embroidery among amateur embroiderers. She must have had quite a following during the earlier part of the century, editing many small magazines on crafts, including knitting, crochet, tatting and lace making. These were produced in conjunction with *Woman's Magazine* and *The Girl's Own Paper* of which she was the editor.

She was a keen needlewoman in the realm of plain sewing and an interested embroiderer, but a journalist, not an artist, although she had some art school training. She was prolific in her editing, in writing many novels and books on practical subjects and in 1912 produced *Stitchery*, a quarterly magazine at sixpence per copy. As stitchery annuals containing the four copies of the previous year, these were sold up until the early twenties and maybe later; numbers 37 to 40 were published as volume 10 at the end of 1922.

In most of the books on design published in the first decade of the twentieth century the embroiderer received quite sound advice, still applicable today, but the application of richer fabrics to poorer seems to have been repeated as necessary instruction: 'Silk may be placed on linen or canvas, wool on linen or even silk on silk, and linen on linen; she must never place linen or wool threads on silk'. Outline darning in which the background was covered in close stitches with the pattern left plain, was popular; a broad surface, bold lines and pure, brilliant colouring was advocated and a warning given 'not to squander fine and delicate work on a banner or wall hanging, you will only make it niggling and ineffective. . . . Good taste in colour can only be acquired by the study of nature. . . . A valuable device for correcting a want of harmony between two adjoining masses of colour, is an outline of contrasting colour round both, and . . . if possible obtain threads dyed with organic dyes . . . aniline dyes fade . . . their colours are vicious'. Wool embroidery, it was suggested, was most effective worked on a large, bold scale, with 'outline curves filled in with a variety of fanciful stitches'.

International Drawing Congress

It is interesting to read information from an illustrated handbook of the International Drawing Congress in London, published in 1908. A detailed report on embroidery and other crafts was given of a retrospective exhibition of the Board of Education examinations. Work done by students awarded gold and silver medals in the last ten years was shown, the opinion being that there was a great advance in design for craft work and manufacturers. This was due to the acceptance of actual objects rather than work on paper. An advance in embroidery was noted, with mention of particular schools: 'the Camberwell school does excellent work in design for embroidery' and 'from Leeds there are admirable examples in embroidery. The improved teaching which has brought about these local results . . . is due to inspiration and reasoned ideals of the Royal College of Art. . . . A supply of brilliant young teachers goes out continually to provincial schools'. The article gave a short note on the Royal College of Art saying that it was primarily intended for teachers and students, selected by competition in the art examinations of the Board of Education. In the school of ornament and design there were three considerations: a knowledge of the crafts, a study of tradition and of nature and practical craft classes. Museum study depended on particular interests and was adapted to present day design, while nature study was a most necessary part of the training. Embroidery became one of the specialised crafts in the College after Grace Christie was appointed in 1909 to teach embroidery.

Summary 1900–1910

Prominent people

M H Baillie Scott

Grace Christie

Marguerite Randall

W Paulson Townsend

Flora Klickmann

Societies, schools, exhibitions, events

1900	Northumberland Handicraft Guild
1901	Samplers – exhibition
	Arts and Crafts Exhibition Society – continuing shows
1902	Coronation of Edward VII and Queen Alexandra
1902	Exhibition in Turin – Jessie Newbery and Ann Macbeth showed work
1903	Arts and Crafts exhibition society – seventh exhibition
1903	Competition of the Worshipful Company of Broderers
1905	English Embroidery exhibition
1906	Society of Certificated Embroideresses formed

Main types of embroidery

Early 1900s

Flat appliqué

Copying of historic embroideries

Canvas embroideries

Ideas based on peasant costume

Embroidery in beads and metal threads on costume

Art needlework continues

Embroidery using the human figure

Silk embroidery

Advanced embroidery by the Glasgow School of Art

Art needlwork transfers popular

Peacocks, allegorical and historical subjects favoured

Larger embroidered hangings seen

Quilting still popular

Magazines and books

1900	*Art and Needlework*, Lewis F Day
1901	*Samplers and Tapestries*, Marius Huish
1906	*Embroidery and Tapestry Weaving*, Grace Christie
1906 –55	*Fancy Needlework Illustrated*
1908 –09	*Embroidery* (magazine) Grace Christie
1907 –10	*Needlecraft Monthly*

26 1900. Part of a border on a fine white linen runner, which could have been a fair linen cloth. Both ends are embroidered with the same patterns in pulled work, needleweaving and drawn thread work. The detail shown repeats the tree shape four more times, with five different fillings, while each pair of leaves has a similar pattern. The edges of the shapes are whipped, the embroidery executed in fine linen thread. 7 in. × 30 in. (17.8 cm × 76 cm)

27 Possibly late nineteenth century – Jessie Newbery. Part of a cushion cover designed by Jessie Newbery and worked by Edith Rowat. The cover is in unbleached linen, embroidered in crewel wools in greens, pinks, yellow and pale turquoise with a turquoise woollen fringe. Stitches include straight stitch, running, satin and french knots. 28 in. (71 cm) square. Shown at the 1916 exhibition of the Glasgow School of Art. *In the collection of the Glasgow School of Art*

28 1900 – Jessie Newbery. A cushion cover, designed and worked by her on unbleached linen, embroidered in crewel wools in blues, greens, pinks, white, fawn and yellow in long and short stitch, satin and stem with border in needleweaving. 22 in. × 19¼ in. (55.8 cm × 48.9 cm). Published in *The Studio* magazine Vol. IXIX p.235. *The Museum and Art Gallery, Glasgow*

29 Early twentieth century – Jessie Newbery. A collar designed and worked by her on a deep rose velvet, embroidered in pink silks in two thicknesses. Applied rectangles of dark grey velvet are sewn with semi-circular and pear-shaped glass beads in two greens. French knots, buttonhole and couching are used for the decoration. 24 in. × 8½ in. (60.9 cm × 21 cm) from neck to hem. *The Museum and Art Gallery, Glasgow*

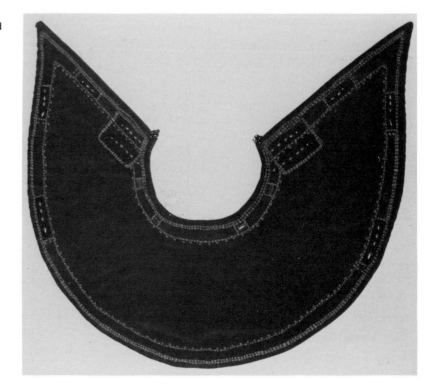

30 Above: 1900. A panel on mid-green satin, embroidered in untwisted floss silks. The birds are in blues and tans to pale mauves; the leaves are in dull, autumn colours of mauves, tans and greens. A couched ground with mainly long and short stitch. *Embroiders' Guild*

31 Below: Early twentieth century – Jessie Newbery. A belt designed and worked by her, in blue linen, embroidered in silk threads in grey, pale blue and fawn. Couching, french knots and needleweaving, with large 'milky' glass beads and a metal clasp, complete the belt which measures 2 in. × 26 in. (5 cm × 66 cm). *The Museum and Art Gallery, Glasgow*

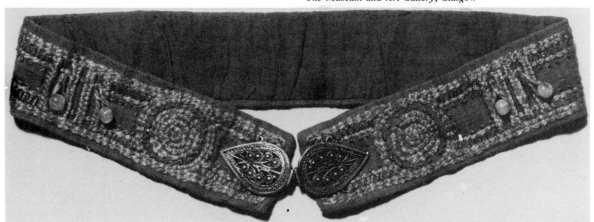

CONFORTAMINI ET AFFERTE
NOBIS DE FRVCTIBVS TERRÆ

32 Above: 1900 – Godfrey Blount. A panel in dark natural linen, with linen applied fabrics, possibly hand-dyed. The leaves are in yellow-green, grey-green and a lightish olive green. The apples are light green, the grapes grey, tan, grey blue and a greyish fawn. The dark garment is brown, the other a light fawn, as is the flesh. The hair is yellow green. The trunks and lettering are in the lightish olive green. The embroidery is entirely in satin stitch in a slate blue linen thread, varying from $\frac{1}{8}$ in. (3 mm) to almost $\frac{1}{4}$ in. (6 mm) in width. 61 in. $\times 85\frac{1}{2}$ in. (154.5 cm $\times$ 219 cm). *Victoria and Albert Museum, London*

33 Right: 1900. One panel of a screen consisting of five panels, each worked with a similar design showing a strong art nouveau influence. The background fabric is of natural linen, with silk embroidery in tans and pale tans, grey-greens and green merging to cream. Stitches include couching and long and short stitch. *The Embroiderers' Guild*

34 Far right: 1895–1902 – Phoebe Traquair. One panel of four from the Denys Series inspired by Denys l'Auxerrois in Walter Pater's *Imaginary Portraits*. The panels are each 88 in. $\times 36$ in. (224 cm $\times 91$ cm) and depict allegorical scenes. The panel illustrated, the fourth, is 'Victory, ultimate salvation through higher powers, rather than by the merits of the individual'. The embroidery covers the ground completely. Cream stem stitch is used for the flesh, the vines are in pinks and greens, the wings in pinks and reds. The leopard skin is cream with spots in ginger and brown. The rainbow is worked in colours to give an effect of transparency. Gold thread is used for the halo. *National Galleries of Scotland, Edinburgh*

37 Below: 1901 – Ann Macbeth. The other side of the banner for the British Association of the Advancement of Science, for Professor Rucker, president of the Association for the year. Appliqué in natural linen on dark greyish-brown linen. On the coat-of-arms the figure is in green with yellow hair, with satin stitch and couched outlines in dull, pale turquoise silk. Three shells on black contain a yellow band in between them. The lions are pink, the helmet and wrap in real colours; satin stitch, stem stitch and straight stitches are used with some metal thread. The border consists of blue-green and cream rectangles in satin stitch. *The British Association for the Advancement of Science*

35 Left: 1901 – George Frederick Bodley. Cope made by the Embroiderers' Guild of St Paul's, Knightsbridge. The background is of red silk damask, with appliqué of crimson velvet, gold cord, green silk and canvas. The embroidery is in gold thread, gold cord and silk in green, red, yellow and brown, in laid work, couching and *or nué* with metal spangles. Fleur-de-lys, sunbursts, stylized pineapples and lettering under the crown form the decoration. In St Paul's, Knightsbridge. *Photo: Victoria and Albert Museum, London*

36 Above: 1901 – Jessie Newbery. One side of a banner for the British Association for the Advancement of Science. Applied linen on linen, natural colour on a darker, greyish linen with a green tree and mantling in green and natural. The fish are of mauvish pink linen. Satin stitch is used for the lettering and outlines. The Bishop is in realistic colours. Other colours used are blue, grey, purple, pink. The embroidery is in floss silk. *The British Association for the Advancement of Science*

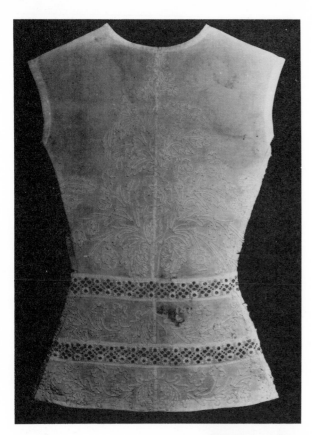

38 Left: Early twentieth century. The back of a bodice in white piqué, with braid decoration applied by hand. Insets are in machine embroidery

40 Top right: Early twentieth century – probably by Ann Macbeth. A pair of blue silk curtains with black silk borders. Appliqué in beige silk, embroidered in floss silk in black, green and cream, in satin, running and stem stitches, with some couching. *In the collection of the Glasgow School of Art*

41 Bottom right: A detail of the curtain containing the flower. *The Glasgow School of Art*

39 Right: Early twentieth century – Ann Macbeth. A cushion cover designed and worked by her. The cover is in unbleached linen, embroidered in silks in pinks, green and blue. Stitches include satin, straight stitch, flat stitches and french knots with some couching. Round glass beads are included. 22 in. (55.8 cm) square. *The Museum and Art Gallery, Glasgow*

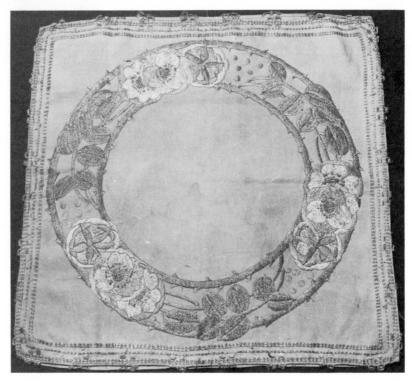

42 Top left: 1902 – Queen Alexandra's coronation dress. Detail – the dress of gold tissue is covered with white net, embroidered in gold spangles and gold and silver floral sprays. Lady Curzon, wife of the Viceroy of India, supervised the embroidery. *The London Museum*

43 Far left: 1902 – Queen Alexandra's coronation gloves. Of white kid, containing the crown and royal ciphers on the backs. Coiling gold stems and leaves decorate the sleeves of the gloves, which are lined with purple velvet and edged with gold lacing. The gloves were made by the King's glove maker, Messrs Harborow, New Bond Street. *The London Museum*

44 Left: 1902 – Queen Mary's dress and train. Worn at the coronation of Edward VII, when she was Princess of Wales. The train has a design of wreaths and flowers in vases, on gold and silver strip (plate) gold thread spangles and diamanté. The train was made by Frederic, by special appointment to Her Majesty Queen Alexandra and by special appointment to HRH the Princess of Wales. *The London Museum*

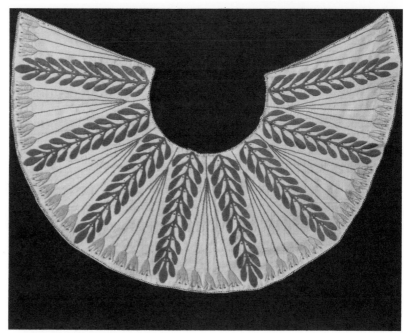

45 Top: 1902. A detail of the dress worn by Queen Mary as Princess of Wales, at the coronation of Edward VII. The dress is in cream satin with rich embroidery in gold thread and pearl festoons, with mimosa sprays in gold and pearl appliqué, gold thread, spangles and diamanté. *The London Museum*

46 Bottom: 1903 – M H Baillie Scott. A collar of natural shantung, with leaves in green satin stitch and flowers in bright, light blue satin stitch. Mauve stem-stitch stems and small silver beads with a black and cream braid around the edge of the collar, complete the embroidery. This collar may have been worked by M H Baillie Scott's wife. 21 in. × 7½ in. (53.3 cm × 18.7 cm). *Victoria and Albert Museum, London*

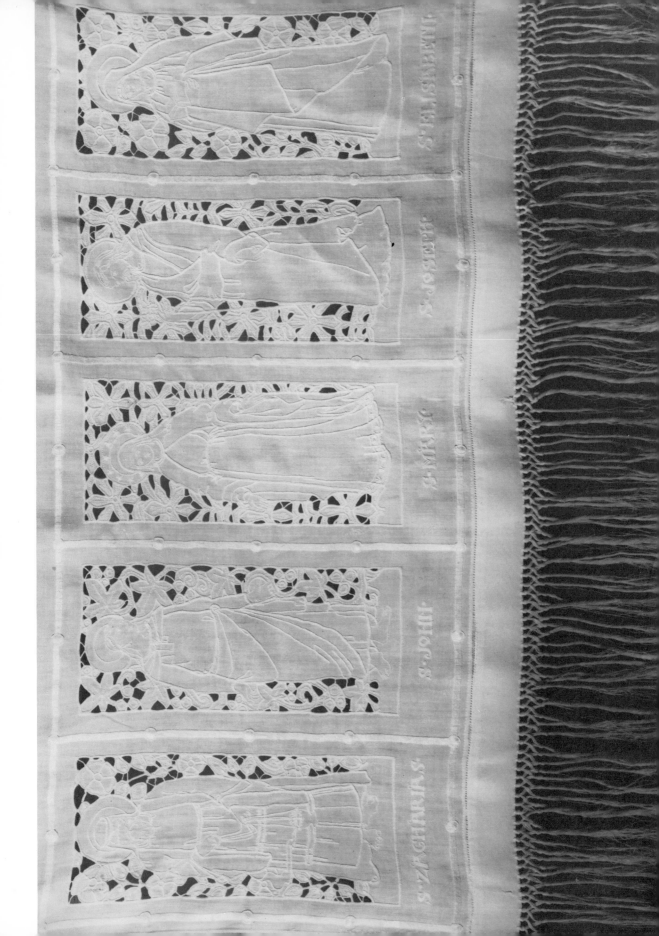

47 Left: 1905 – A fair linen cloth. In fine white linen, with both ends embroidered in the same pattern. Cut work using buttonhole, back, and stem stitches, with satin stitch bands to divide the panels which are worked in fine white linen threads. *St Mary's Convent, Wantage*

48 Right: 1905 – A detail of the fair linen cloth. Each panel is contained within a satin stitch frame with the name of the saint embroidered solidly in stem stitch and is 8 in. × 3¾ in. (20 cm × 9.4 cm) in size. *St Mary's Convent, Wantage*

49 About 1905 – a hanging. One of a pair worked by the Royal School of Art Needlework, on a boldly patterned silk brocade of dull yellow on a cream ground. The embroidery is in crewel wools and stranded silk, probably filoselle. The flowers are heavily padded and the petals are in dark to pale pinks and apricot wools with cream silk highlights. The leaves are in yellow-green silk with wools in grey-greens, dark and light greens, also bottle greens, brownish-greens and some dull blue greens. The stems are in dull pinks, browns, ochre yellows and other colours. The stitches are long and short. The curtain is from Fanhams Hall. 87 in. × 120 in. (221 cm × 305 cm). *Victoria and Albert Museum, London*

50 1905 – Margaret MacDonald. One of four panels for a lampshade, in white silk, with applied black ribbons and green silk braid, also pink and green silk fabrics. Clear glass beads are applied too. The lampshade was made for Hill House, Helensburg and was designed by Charles Rennie Mackintoch, the architect, to whom Margaret MacDonald was married. One panel is in the Museum and Art Gallery, Glasgow, another in the Victoria and Albert Museum, London.

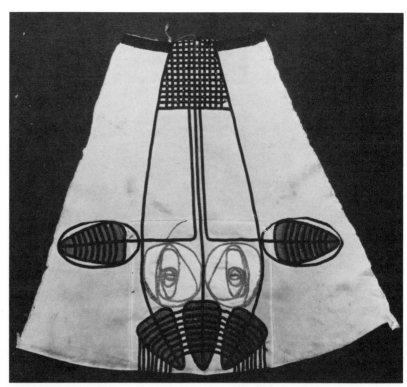

51 1900–1910 – The Leek Embroidery Society. A fragment, on dark, natural tussah silk, in soft white, several shades of turquoise, pink, light and mid reds and gold threads, much worn away. The scroll shapes are outlined in heavier thread in red floss silk. Stitches include stem, buttonhole and couching. Worked over a printed pattern by Thomas Wardle. Width of fabric $3\frac{1}{2}$ in. (9 cm). The embroidery measures $5\frac{3}{8}$ in. $\times 3\frac{1}{4}$ in. (13.8 cm $\times$ 8 cm). *Gawthorpe Hall*

**52 1909 – Muriel Boyd. A panel signed MB. The ground is
cream silk satin embroidered in coloured floss silks in greens,
brown, pink, purple and white. Stitches include satin, stem,
french knots, knot stitch and straight stitches. Beads in clear
glass are incorporated. The dress is outlined in knot stitch. The
underskirt is in white satin stitch. $18 \times 8\frac{1}{2}$ in. (45 cm $\times$ 21.3 cm).**
The Museum and Art Gallery, Glasgow

53 Left: 1909 – Mabel Nicholls. 'Te Deum Laudamus'. Panel for the front of an organ worked in floss silks, with the garments stitched in couched and laid work to create the patterns. Mabel Nicholls designed and executed her own embroideries. She gained four national awards for embroidery from South Kensington and a 'diplome d'honneur' and three bronze medals from the Concours International des arts de la femme in Paris. She also exhibited with the Arts and Crafts Society

54 Right: Twentieth century. A detail of a Durham quilt showing the typical feather patterns of the north of England. *Victoria and Albert Museum, London*

55 Below: 1908. A design by Frank Newbery, presumably for an altar frontal

The second decade of the twentieth century

English Secular Embroidery was written in 1910 by Mary Jourdain who felt that there was an interest in secular work as well as in ecclesiastical embroidery, as seen in the splendid exhibition of 1905. In the schools of art, embroidery for the church, for dress and for household articles had been the main occupation of students studying the craft. The development of ideas rather than techniques was increasing, and a student in an art school in 1910 remembers the excitement of another student on being told that she could embroider a pictorial hanging as a change from her embroidery on dress and her ecclesiastical work, which were often based on previous styles.

In 1910 the work of **Miss H Harvey** was reviewed in *Needlecraft Monthly* magazine. She was trained in Italy as a painter and carried out a number of ecclesiastical embroideries at the end of the nineteenth century and the beginning of the twentieth century. George Bodley designed a cope for the Bishop of London, which she worked. The Reverend Ernest Geldart, the Rector of Lesser Braxted, Essex, designed many of the pieces carried out by Miss Harvey, including a frontal for Chislehurst, her first commission, from Canon Murray. Later she carried out a banner for Chislehurst. One of her best works was a banner for Chichester Cathedral, containing figures about 42 in. (106 cm) high, taking up almost a third of the complete size. The architectural features were worked entirely in gold. Miss Harvey had to earn her living and became one of the best embroiderers in the country, although for the most part she carried out other people's designs; among these were frontals for St Barnabas Church, Walthamstow, designed by Mr Carol, the diocesan architect for Lincoln. A banner for Brompton Oratory was another outstanding example of her embroidery.

Roger Fry introduced the first exhibition of French post-impressionists to England in 1910, while the Russian Ballet took Paris by storm.

The Russian Ballet

Bakst's designs for the Russian Ballet in 1909–10 and Poiret's *haute-couture* creations, derived from his interest in eastern costumes, influenced the dress at this time in Europe and later in England. However, embroidery in England seemed to be unaffected by the excitement in Paris which had been created by the flamboyance of the oriental colours and patterns of eastern extraction, hitherto unknown in the West and seen first on the stage and later in Poiret's salon. However, as Paris eventually influenced English styles, the trends in France should be mentioned. Chanel was fascinated by the brilliance of the ballet and designed garments with beautiful embroidery in beads and silk threads. Gold and silver lace was seen on elaborate evening outfits and the richness of the Orient continued to be an inspiration during the war years in Paris.

Coronation robes and costume

The coronation of George V in 1911 followed the pattern of the previous coronation, the King wearing robes similar to those worn in 1902. The Queen's robe resembled that worn by Queen Alexandra, embroidered with emblems of the British Empire. The design by Jessie Robinson was carried out by the Ladies' Work Society. Her dress was in cream satin, embroidered in gold threads, again with emblems of the British Empire, bordered round the hem with a pattern representing waves of the oceans which connected the British Empire. The Queen's dressmakers Messrs Reville and Rossiter made the dress, and the embroidery was designed by Jessie Robinson who supervised the work (pages 77, 78).

A description of one of the dresses worn by the six trainbearers to Queen Mary says that the dress was of cream satin, the centre front panel decorated with beads worked in a trellis pattern, with a large butterfly in applied pearl beads over the bust, and a similar butterfly at the centre front hem and on the short net sleeves (London Museum catalogue *Coronation Costume 1685–1953*).

An interesting panel owned by Helen Grundy was worked in 1913 by Emily Cannon, her grandmother, who met Lucy, the sister of Walter Crane, at boarding school and through her came the influence of William Morris (page 80). One of the amusements allowed Emily Cannon as a child was embroidery, which she continued to pursue as an adult. She painted her designs in water colour and sent them to the firm of William Morris and Co, who would return them traced onto linen with the right colours and silks for working the embroidery.

The first public exhibition of the Society of Certificated Embroideresses was held in 1911 and in 1913 new rules were made. They had no permanent meeting place and during the First World War ceased their meetings although individual members kept in touch.

Needle and Thread magazine

Grace Christie edited the magazine *Needle and Thread* in January 1914, which was devoted to the study of fine needlework: pattern making, embroidery in the past, and all other subjects of interest to 'those who could ply daintily, needle and thread'. Unfortunately it was discontinued during the war but the articles in the four copies published were excellent. Selwyn Image wrote: 'A few thoughts on designing for embroidery: embroidery is an art and craft: *art* – imaginative design, *craft* – how to use the needle and thread. Design at its best is largely determined by the material and process in and through which it is to be carried out'. He explained the points of design in relation to the distance from which the embroidery is viewed and said: 'Texture is important and depends largely on effective variation of stitch. If the designer and worker are one, it will determine stitches as work proceeds'.

Dress embroidery, 1914

At this time Dorothy Larcher, a textile designer of some note, in an account of dress design and embroidery in *Needle and Thread* said:

'There are several ways of adorning dresses with embroidery, all-over patterns, borders, or else concentrated in one place such as the collar, sleeves or vest to let in. . . . In floral designs shading should generally be avoided. . . . This will cause a muddled effect when the material is draped. The realistic treatment of flowers on design for dress embroidery is unsuitable, because the idea to be conveyed is not that the person is decorated with real flowers . . . but rather the design should have a life of its own. The number of different stitches used in one piece of work should be limited . . . the same due regard to colour. . . . A design in two or even three colours or even one is very effective. If the dress be black, white or any neutral tint, any number of bright colours can be used with care . . . white on white. . . . Colours should be clear, not of the muddy kind generally known as "art" shades'.

Advertisements

During the period prior to 1920 and excluding the War, there were many advertisements for embroidery and embroidery materials, which suggest that the craft was popular. As examples, the Royal School of Art Needlework in 1908 advertised 'every variety of article most delicately worked', and 'a very large stock of traced work always ready, commenced if desired'. An advertisement in 1914 by the firm of William Morris and Co stated that embroideries and embroidery materials were dyed with pure vegetable colours like those used in ancient work. They also reproduced designs by William Morris. Firms advertised private lessons in 'church embroidery and all kinds of fancy needlework'. Individuals who taught on their own premises seemed to abound at this time, teaching design, copying old designs, mounting, enlarging and reducing drawings. An advertisement by Miss Mary Symonds stated that she was a tapestry restorer and embroideress to His Majesty the King and that embroidery of all descriptions was worked or traced and prepared for working. The 'sampler series' of coloured cards designed by Grace Christie contained 'actual embroideries reproduced in colour', with drawings showing other applications of the designs and particulars of transfers. These cards, six in number, were (1) Autumn leaves, (2) London Pride, (3) Blackberries, (4) Wild flowers, (5) Carnations, (6) English Birds and were all published by Pearsall and Company and advertised in several magazines before the War.

Exhibition of ecclesiastical work

An exhibition in the Glasgow School of Art in 1916 caused great interest, as it was the first exhibition of ancient and modern ecclesiastical embroideries ever held in the School: Jessie Newbery and Ann Macbeth helped to arrange this exhibition which contained, besides the work of earlier periods, contemporary examples by Helen Gorrie from Edinburgh, Doris Taylor and others from Manchester, and designs by May Morris, Charles Ricketts and Ann Macbeth, as well as those from the firm of William Morris and Co. By all accounts the work was magnificent, but the exhibition contained more old than new embroidery.

Well-known embroiderers

Embroiderers well-known during the earlier part of the century are referred to here, although their work spanned several decades and may be referred to again in Volume 2.

Ida Marion Dight was trained in a wide field of arts and crafts, including drawing, design, dress design and embroidery. Nature drawing and museum study were a part of her course. She specialised in embroidery and its various branches, and also in dressmaking, in order to understand the design and decoration of garments.

She was awarded several scholarships and attended drawing classes for prospective teachers. Before taking up a teaching post she worked in the trade and in 1907 was recognised as a teacher of embroidery by the City and Guilds of London Institute. In 1919 she was given leave to work with Messrs Reville and Rossiter, dressmakers, to learn the uses of embroidery in the trade and to visit dressmaking firms and workrooms.

She went to Paris in 1924, to study the methods of two trade schools, where she found them working more or less on the same lines as those in London. Students from 13 to 15 years of age took a general and a professional course for two years, after which they sat for an examination, those with special aptitudes for the branches of the trade in which they had chosen to work being allowed an extra year's study.

In 1928 and 1930 she was awarded prizes for industrial design. The Royal Society of Arts commented on her 1928 design for an eight-colour Jacobean block for 50 in. (127 cm) wide linen saying 'although based on a well known Jacobean embroidery, it shows originality in treatment without departing from the characteristics of English seventeenth-century design. The design is well conceived and skilfully adapted'.

Ida Dight was an excellent teacher of machine embroidery and wrote an article on machine embroidery in 1934 for the magazine *Embroidery*. She also wrote a book on the same subject.

Louisa Pesel studied with Lewis F Day. She devoted her life to furthering the cause of embroidery and started the West Riding Needlework Association where she aimed at high standards of work. In 1903 she was appointed as the designer to the Royal Hellenic School of Needlework and Lace in Athens, where she was the director until 1907. The school flourished and provincial centres were started in Greece, the work produced in the schools being sent to the United States and European capitals. She was commissioned by the Victoria and Albert Museum to work samplers of stitches from historic English embroideries. These were published in colour by Lund Humphries in 1912. In 1913 two more portfolios of stitches appeared, one from eastern embroideries and one from western embroideries. These were given to the Victoria and Albert Museum, London.

Louisa Pesel was appointed as an Extra Inspector of Art Needlework and so was able to instruct teachers, giving many lectures on embroidery. During the war she was in her home town, Bradford, where she helped to start a handicraft section for shell-shocked soldiers in the Khaki Club.

When in 1920 the Society of Certificated Embroideresses became the Embroiderers' Guild, Louisa Pesel became its President for two years, and taught classes on colour balance. She wrote an article on colour and form which was published in the magazine *Embroidery*. The article provoked many letters of disagreement and in her published reply to these letters, she said that if it was admitted that embroidery was an art, stitching 'could no more be the chief consideration than is brushwork in painting' and also that 'an extreme technical proficiency is almost inevitably the death of the artistic spirit'. She started portfolios for members on the uses of stitches and added to those portfolios already in use. She moved to Weymouth, and in 1925 to Twyford, Hants, where she established a thriving embroidery centre – The Yew Tree Industries. Workers used six stitches only until these were mastered, working on linen and making small articles, then when proficient they were able to select their own stitches. Later, informal tests were given to those wishing to join the industry. Work was exhibited but repeats of a piece were discouraged in order to avoid monotony and to keep variety of outlook. Designs were adapted from seventeenth-century whitework samplers, and were worked in double running, pulled stitches and geometric satin stitch. On the influence of materials and stitches on design she said 'Designers of embroidery must have some knowledge of materials and stitches . . .'. She organised a communal piece of work with the local Women's Institute and with Sybil Blunt carried out the canvas embroideries for Winchester Cathedral, with the aid of a group of women whose skills were hitherto unknown. They started with small articles such as kneelers and almsbags, worked in stitches seen on Elizabethan bags and samplers, but in wools, instead of silks. This was an important development in ecclesiastical embroidery. (Pages 106, 107, 117.)

Louisa Chart was a founder member of the Society of Certificated Embroideresses. She taught in Wimbledon and Kingston-on-Thames Schools of Art, then was appointed to the staff of Edinburgh College of Art, where she inspired many students with her teaching. In the college, design was carried out in the design room, while she taught techniques. Her keen interest in history and her enthusiasm for teaching the history of embroidery was such that her students acquired a lasting regard for embroidery as well as excellent technique.

She possessed a wide knowledge of the craft and its conservation and undertook the repair of old works, among them the Oxburg hangings, the Loch Leven hangings and of embroideries in Holyroodhouse where Dorothy Angus, one of her students, assisted her. A number of exhibitions were organised by her, including the first one held by the Needlework Development Scheme in 1934 which was shown in the four Scottish schools of art. After this she travelled to Europe, buying embroideries for the scheme. Her own work was lively, with rich textures of stitchery and among other embroideries she worked a set of canvas chair covers for the Palace of Holyroodhouse, a bible cover for King Edward VII and a heraldic coat of arms for George Watson's Boys' College. Her nephew, an architect, often drew out designs for her, which were worked by herself and her sister. A student, Margaret Blow, who was attending the Diploma course in needlework at Athol Crescent College of Domestic Science, Edinburgh, during the war years, said that between 1943 and 1944, students taking needlework and design for the Diploma attended Louisa Chart's classes at the College of Art. Another student, Wynn Phillipson, studied embroidery full-time at the Edinburgh College of Art. She found Louisa Chart a knowledgeable and inspiring teacher.

Constance Brown started to teach in Cambridge at the School of Art in 1912 and was considered an excellent and inspiring teacher who did a great deal for her students, one of whom was Rosamund Willis. Her work was mentioned in a number of reviews of exhibitions; in the British Institute of Industrial Art Exhibition at the Victoria and Albert Museum in 1922 she showed 'charming canvas pictures'. She was noted as being an 'excellent stitcher' and wrote many articles for *Embroidery* and *The Embroideress* magazines. She designed several transfer designs of bunches and vases of flowers for embroidery magazines and carried out canvas panels and other embroideries herself.

Eve Simmons studied painting with Walter Sickert. Although she had no formal training in embroidery, she developed a definite style of her own. She began to embroider in the First World War, and produced some charming smocks for children. Her first smock (page 83) was shown at the Arts and Crafts Exhibition Society and at the Grosvenor Gallery. In 1916 she worked a large hanging now in the Whitworth Gallery, Manchester. Eve Simmons also worked on black linen in white and cream threads, embroidering garments which had great individuality. Her designs were often linear, sometimes in back stitch. It was said in the late twenties that her work was too well known to need comment.

Joan Drew appears to have been self-taught and although little is known about her early life, she did illustrate several books in her youth. She was also known for her lettering. From research by Joan Edwards it seems that she was a keen embroiderer from an early age. During the First World War she designed and made a number of banners for the village hall, Blackheath (page 76). In 1920 she taught the first embroidery classes in the Victoria and Albert Museum, these being the outcome of Ann Macbeth's and Margaret Swanson's *Educational Needlecraft*. She was a friend of Mary Symonds (Mrs Antrobus), Louisa Pesel, Josephine Newall and the Honourable Rachel Kay Shuttleworth, who possessed some of her work at Gawthorpe Hall. (Colour plate 3.)

Joan Drew held private classes in her own studio; she also taught children and did a great deal for the Women's Institutes. She published portfolios of designs for embroidery, adapted from historic examples, but simplified for those who were unable to design. These were well drawn and presented. One article she wrote on embroidered flowers included simple motifs to be arranged as the worker wished but to be embroidered in fine silk or cotton. She exhibited frequently, one banner for the Winchcombe Musical Festival being described as 'elaborate and beautiful in design, worked all over in flat stitch in vegetable dyed wools'. In fact she was mentioned frequently as exhibiting good work, showing banners and hangings and sometimes rugs. She wrote a number of articles for *The Embroideress* and *Embroidery* magazines. She also taught at the Embroiderers' Guild and exhibited with them. By all accounts she was a prolific worker, designing and executing embroideries both for secular and ecclesiastical purposes, and also designing the portfolios of ideas for those who wished to use them.

Kathleen Harris (née Kathleen Turner) was a pioneer in teaching both young people and adults. For a short time she taught at Camberwell Art School, then at the Girls' Trade School for Dressmaking, London. She later became head of embroidery at the Manchester Municipal College of Art where she taught all ages. It was said of her that no one could have taken a more active part in the recent movement towards the resumption through the schools of the English tradition of good needlework (*The Studio* July 1922). An article by R Dawson says 'in recent years decorative and constructive needlework . . . has been recognised not only as a valuable means of general education, but as a craft through which deftness of fingers and a discriminating taste can become valuable assets'. She was an innovator in using striped, checked and spotted fabrics for pattern building, long before these were introduced in other educational establishments. Her aim in Manchester was to teach all forms of needlework. Students were encouraged to study history, as the College and the Whitworth Art Gallery between them possessed a large collection of historic embroideries and lace. Slides were borrowed from the Victoria and Albert Museum as a supplement to these studies. She said 'Embroidery, or Needlework, as I prefer to call it, is taught as an advanced subject and is a limitless craft'. The students tackled everything from simple articles and garments to advanced figure subjects for ecclesiastical embroidery, at first omitting samplers as Kathleen Harris thought these of little value until a standard of technique was obtained. She had her own department and although students attended lectures in the design room, practical work was carried out in the embroidery room. Students of different age groups and abilities attended her classes; social workers, certificate students, and girls of 14 to 15 years of age were among these. Criticisms of designs and homework were given. Notebooks on the history and practice of the craft were kept and students were encouraged to try out a variety of materials and methods. They undertook commissions and received instruction on conservation. While in Manchester Kathleen Harris trained many teachers and was regarded in the north of England as the authority on design and embroidery, influencing many people who turned to her for advice. In 1921 she took Grace Christie's place at the Royal College of Art, London, where she taught part-time until the Second World War. She exhibited with Dorothy Larcher and Phyllis Barron, both well known textile designers. This exhibition was the nucleus of what became the Red Rose Guild in Manchester in 1920, starting with a show in Houldsworth Hall. The exhibition consisted of local artists, some from London and other parts of the country, and in 1921, owing to much interest shown in the work, the Red Rose Guild of Artworkers was formed, with a membership of 20. It retained its base in Manchester.

Kathleen Harris was an excellent draughtswoman; her work was mainly floral in style, distinctive and always finely drawn, sensitive and with excellent technique. She was willing to impart any knowledge that could be of help to students and treated them as individuals, encouraging their particular interests. Apart from her speciality she had a fund of knowledge useful to the young student, was always a good judge and critic, but found it difficult to understand the low standard of embroidery in exhibitions in comparison with other crafts. For 20 years at the Regent Street Polytechnic she trained students for the City and Guilds of London Institute examinations in embroidery and for the National Diploma in Design. (Pages 101, 109, 119, 163.)

Mary Ozanne, although rarely designing embroidery, carried out many commissions from architects' designs. She was also a conservationist and repaired many ecclesiastical vestments, including the coronation copes in the cathedrals of Durham and Wells in 1902. Between 1935 and 1974 she worked in London and Sawbridgeworth. She carried out work for architects such as Stephen Dykes Bower, Laurence Bond and George Pace and was particularly interested in beautiful materials for embroidery. As she had a good business relationship with the clergy she had a great number of commissions and worked for many cathedrals, including Canterbury, Durham, York, St Pauls and others. She made copes for the Archbishop of Canterbury when he was Bishop of Durham, then of York, and two or more when he became Archbishop of Canterbury. She also carried out a number of commissions for churches in the USA. Her work was technically excellent and she was usually in great demand.

Dorothy Angus was in Aberdeen for 35 years where she taught at Grays School of Art. She was a brilliant teacher and had a strong influence on embroidery in north-east Scotland. She had intended to paint, but decided that there was a better chance of earning a living by learning about crafts. She studied embroidery with Louisa Chart who gave her a sound training in techniques and history of embroidery.

Dorothy Angus helped Louisa Chart in the restoration of embroideries in the Palace of Holyroodhouse, this being instrumental in her appointment to the Carnegie Trust Craft School in Dunfermline as an assistant teacher of embroidery in 1916. There the teachers drew the designs and the students worked them stitch by stitch, as the school was for amateurs and local people, for whom recreational activities were provided. In 1920 she went to Grays School of Art, where she found embroidery at a low level of attainment. With her lively approach she was able to raise the standards in the use of colour and design in the craft, the concepts of which were pictorial at that time. Kathleen Whyte, one of her students, felt that the results were rather Persian in style. Large hangings of figure compositions, darned into evenweave fabrics in wools in a variety of patterns became popular. Her classes were full, and her collaboration with James Hamilton, the head of the design department and a brilliant teacher, led to some most exciting work being produced, in which the quality was similar to that found in large tapestries. This led to an interest in the link between drawing and stitchery. (Page 122.)

Dorothy Angus exhibited with the Modern Embroidery Society in Edinburgh and with the Society of Scottish Artists. She was interested particularly in the relationship of threads to materials, often working on strongly textured grounds with which these threads merged, giving an impression of a subject rather than a clear definition. There was also a period when she used smooth fabrics such as linen and shantung, stitching on these in silk threads or soft cottons. Many of her ideas contained figures, although her subjects were varied and one of her commissions was to make a heraldic bedspread for Lord Glentar where really sumptuous materials were used (Kathleen Whyte, *Embroidery* Autumn 1973). She did a great deal for Scottish embroidery and for her students. Most of Dorothy Angus's work is privately owned; the 'War Impressions' is to be given eventually to the Royal Scottish Museum, Edinburgh. She said when writing to Rosamund Angus in February 1977: 'You must know that I do not consider myself in the first rank of embroiderers. I would be very stupid not to know that I was an excellent teacher and have inspired several students to go far beyond me'.

Doris Taylor had a thorough training, and was equally as good a painter as an embroiderer, in which subject she showed excellent technical ability. She learned embroidery first of all with Kathleen Harris, and at the Royal College of Art she was taught by Grace Christie, some of her embroidery being published in *Samplers and Stitches*. She was, however, a very versatile artist, having studied enamelling, writing and illumination, with woodcarving as a major subject. After gaining her diploma at the College, she taught design and crafts at Hastings School of Art for two years, then was appointed to Kathleen Harris's post at the Manchester Municipal School of Art in charge of dress and embroidery. She taught there until her retirement. Doris Taylor was an excellent teacher and prepared students for the Board of Education examinations in Industrial Design, in Dress and Embroidery, and later for the National Diploma in Design, also for the City and Guilds of London Institute examinations. During the 1950s she was an assessor for the Ministry of Education Intermediate Examinations in Art. Under her guidance, commissions were carried out by the students for civic and ecclesiastical purposes. Among these were banners for the Young Australian League, the British Medical Association and the Mothers' Union. Altar frontals were also designed and worked by her, assisted by students. Doris Taylor herself carried out a number of commissions for banners and frontals and exhibited work as a painter. She was meticulous in carrying out her own work, which was strong in drawing and in design, often incorporating lettering (pages 81, 82, 84, 86, 87, 102, 103, 108, 123). She worked a number of machine embroideries and encouraged students to experiment with new materials and ways in which they might be exploited, using hand and machine embroidery for the decoration of dress and other articles.

Another student at the Royal College of Art during the First World War was **Margaret Holden-Jones**, who studied embroidery with Grace Christie. She was also a very versatile artist, a fine draughtswoman and calligrapher and illustrated a book of plant drawings in 1919 (exhibited in the British Museum 1977). In 1922 at an exhibition sponsored by the British Institute of Industrial Art, in the Victoria and Albert Museum, she showed four brooches, each one inch in size; 'wild strawberry', 'daisies', 'pelican' and 'red bird'. They created a sensation as they were in minute petit-point stitch and nothing like their fineness had previously been seen. They were also a novelty because they were embroidered and set in silver, rather than executed entirely in enamel or metal. An example of her work is shown on page 84. Margaret Holden-Jones has taught all her life, mainly pottery and calligraphy, although she has continued to carry out embroidery herself and has conducted occasional classes in the subject. (Page 111).

Rachel Kay Shuttleworth of Gawthorpe Hall should be mentioned here as at this time she cherished an idea that one day she would promote a craft house where the study of textiles could be undertaken. She attended art classes in Paris and gained there a sound knowledge of the history of art and the principles of painting. She always had a strong interest in social welfare and was an instigator of various associations, helping to promote the Civic Arts Centre in the north of England. In order to understand the basic techniques she learnt professional needlework in a workroom and realised that for teaching, visual aids were necessary, so her collection of lace, on which she became an authority, and embroideries, began while she was quite young.

The War years

During the 1914–18 War there was little progress in embroidery in Great Britain although various projects were started by interested embroiderers, to help the wounded soldiers in the hospitals.

A student was sent to Reading to organise needlework for these soldiers, under the auspices of Ann Macbeth who through her efforts also introduced them to the painting of pottery as an occupation while recovering. Louisa Pesel in Bradford did a great deal in encouraging embroidery for the wounded, as did **Ernest Thesiger**, an actor of some repute, who began his art career as a painter but was always keen on embroidery. While recovering from war wounds, he found this occupation was a great comfort. It gave him the idea of starting a scheme for those in hospital, whereby the soldiers worked canvases designed by him. This proved very therapeutic and led to other schemes. He carried out a number of ecclesiastical embroideries and tried a variety of different types of work, experimenting with techniques and design, but his main interest was in canvas work. He remarked in his book *Adventures in Embroidery*, published in 1941, that 'unfortunately much of the work that is produced today is merely a slavish copy of the best work of the seventeenth and eighteenth centuries. Needlework is . . . an outlet for the creative instinct . . . and for it adequately to fulfil this purpose, designer and worker should if possible be one and the same person'.

Guilds and institutes

The Northumberland Handicraft Guild, started in 1900, was instrumental in teaching shell-shocked and disabled soldiers as were other institutions and societies towards the end of the War. In 1913 the Women's Institutes had been founded, and included embroidery in their programmes. During this time and after the War the Townswomen's Guild was inaugurated. Both of these bodies aimed at giving instructions in the crafts and in subjects of general interest to those normally at home. Their classes in embroidery were rather rigid, with a number of rules and the emphasis on technique rather than on design, and so were not so much creative as competent. The Scottish Women's Rural Industries was formed in 1917, with similar aims.

The Design and Industries Association was founded in 1915 by a group of manufacturers, retailers, craftsmen and artists 'to encourage excellence of design and workmanship in British Industry'. The first aim was 'fitness for purpose . . . the essential starting point for reform in design, in view of the general debasement of standards following the Industrial Revolution'.

After the War

The War curtailed many activities, including the meetings of the Society of Certificated Embroideresses. Women took on jobs usually associated with men, such as working in factories, driving ambulances and working on the land. After the War, attitudes changed. Women appreciated their freedom and many obtained paid occupations and became self-supporting, although with less leisure. After a great struggle the vote for women over 30 was gained in 1919. Life and society changed and class distinctions were to an extent broken down. The economic situation became unstable and the Great Depression of the inter-war years created much insecurity.

Between the wars the cinema and the theatre increased in popularity; there was a craze for dancing and a general feeling of gaiety. This was a period of new ideas in art, music and literature, in spite of growing strikes and unemployment.

Various movements started just before and after the War, but except for the work of the few adventurous and original artists these did not affect embroidery. The Omega Workshops were opened in 1913 by Roger Fry to encourage young artists and craftsmen to show their work in exhibitions and to promote an interest in the aesthetics of the crafts. This venture encountered many difficulties and unfortunately the enterprise was closed in 1919. Several artists interested in the venture designed for embroidery after the War, among whom were **Duncan Grant** (page 120) and **Vanessa Bell**, both painters, who helped to change the image of embroidery as a craft. The copying of historic examples had been of prime importance previously, but in the twenties began to assume less significance as a more creative approach to design was emerging, fostered by well known artists, such as Paul Nash and William Tryon.

I remember at the end of the War that my mother embroidered holland dresses for myself and my sisters, using transfers of small flowers worked as borders in bright blue and scarlet linen threads. I loved these dresses but my pride and joy was a dress for my birthday in 1923 in a crushed strawberry coloured fabric, the bodice of which was completely covered with a large basket of flowers in self-coloured perlé cotton. This was obviously a transfer for a square cushion cover but I thought that it was elegant.

Summary 1910–1920

Prominent people

Ida Dight, specialist in machine embroidery

Louisa Pesel

Kathleen Harris

Louisa Chart

Doris Taylor

Dorothy Angus

Dorothy Larcher, textile designer

Joan Drew

Mary Ozanne, conservationist and embroiderer

Margaret Holden-Jones

Rachel Kay Shuttleworth, lace expert and collector of embroidery

Duncan Grant, painter and designer for embroidery

Vanessa Bell, painter and designer for embroidery

Roger Fry, critic and painter who owned Omega Workshops

Ernest Thesiger, actor and embroiderer

Societies, schools, exhibitions, events

1911	Coronation of George V and Queen Mary
1911	First exhibition of Society of Certificated Embroideresses
1913	Women's Institutes founded
1913 –19	Omega Workshops – Roger Fry
1914 –18	First World War

1915 Design and Industries Association

1916 Exhibition of Ancient and Modern Ecclesiastical Embroideries – Glasgow School of Art

1917 Scottish Women's Rural Industries
Townswomen's Guild founded

1917 Exhibition of Children's Work, Omega Workshops

1919 Votes for Women over 30

Main types of embroidery

Influence of Paul Poiret's designs slowly infiltrating to Britain – peg-top skirts, beads, rich fabrics and colours
Coronation robes and costume similar to previous coronation
In the schools of art a stronger development of original design – space filling
Larger hangings
Fine silk embroidery, using floral subjects, worked on silk or linen
Scrolling, all over patterns, on garments and accessories – jackets, small bags
Small pictorial panels, often figurative.
Pictorial samplers – Aesop's fables
Curtailment of activities during the War
After the War a continuation of pre-war styles

Magazines and books

1910 *English Secular Embroidery*, Mary Jourdain

1911 *Educational Needlecraft*, Ann Macbeth and Margaret Swanson

1912 *Stitchery* magazine, Flora Klickmann

1912 *English Historical Embroideries*

1913 *Eastern Embroideries*, Louisa Pesel
Western Embroideries, Louisa Pesel

1914 *Needle and Thread*, Grace Christie

1915 *Elementary Needlework*, Mary Symonds

1919 *The Needlewoman* magazine

Caption overleaf

The embroidered screen reads:

MARY MARY QUITE CONTRARY HOW DOES YOUR GARDEN GROW ⟐ WITH SILVER BELLS & COCKLE SHELLS & PRETTY MAIDS ALL OF A ROW ⟐

56 Previous page: Early twentieth century – Josephine Newall, Fisherton-de-la-Mer Industries. Two mats worked on coarse natural linen, in floss silk. Four-sided stitch and other pulled work stitches are combined with eyelet holes and satin stitch. The edges are in buttonhole loops. The initials CL probably indicate those of the worker. Each $4\frac{1}{4}$ in. (10.8 cm) square. *Loaned by Mrs Judd, Salisbury*

57 1910 – Katherine Powell. A hand screen – *Mary, Mary, Quite Contrary*. Embroidered on fine white gauze, with the back and front equally good in technique. Black backstitch lettering is covered on the reverse side with white close herringbone, to give shadow work on the front. Other stitches are darning, stem stitch, satin and laid work. Colours include greens, blues, ochre and salmon pink. The style is reminiscent of Kate Greenaway's illustrations. The frame is silver. The embroidery was worked around 1910 for the City and Guilds of London Institute examination in embroidery. *Given to the Embroiderers' Guild by Lady Hamilton Fairlie*

58 Above: 1910 – Katherine Powell. Panel on a light bronze linen ground, worked in silks. Trees and peacocks in dull blues, stems in dark to light tans. Buttonhole, seeding, couching, back-stitch, satin and stem stitch are used. The limited colour gives unity. *The Embroiderers' Guild*

59 Below: 1910 – Ann Macbeth. A fan embroidered on white silk gauze in floss silks in pinks, blues and several shades of turquoise. Designed but not worked by Ann Macbeth. Satin and stem are the chief stitches used for the work. *Art Gallery and Museum, Glasgow*

FOR·HOME·AND·COUNTRY

BLACKHEATH·WOMENs·INSTITUTE

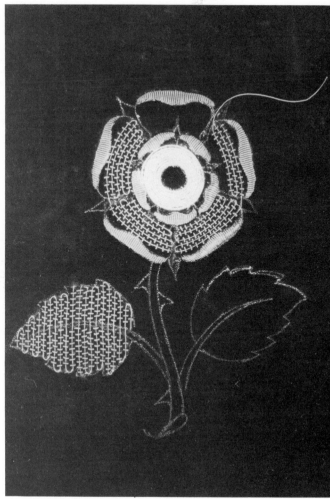

61 Left: 1911. Queen Mary's coronation robe. In purple velvet, embroidered in gold threads by HRH Princess Louise's Ladies' Work Society, for Messrs Warner. The symbolic design contains roses, thistles and shamrocks, growing together on a tree whose branches contain the Queen's initial M and the Imperial Crown which represents the British Empire. The interlocking roots symbolise breadth and complexity. A border of oak leaves and acorns edges the robe. The embroidery was designed and supervised by Jessie Robinson. *The London Museum*

62 Below: 1911. A sample on purple velvet, showing the Tudor Rose in gold threads, worked for the coronation robe. *The London Museum*

60 Left: Early twentieth century – Joan Drew. A Banner. On yellow linen, with the figure in natural linen and a dull mauve linen. The apples are in gold thread, the tree has a brown trunk with black satin outlines. Green blues on a dull green linen are outlined in satin stitch. The lettering is mauve on yellow and yellow on mauve. The banner was made for the new village hall in Blackheath, Hampshire, about 1910–1912. *The Embroiderers' Guild*

63 Above: 1911. A detail of the coronation dress, on white satin.
The London Museum

**64 Top right: 1911. One of Queen Mary's coronation shoes,
designed by Jessie Robinson. White kid, embroidered with a rose,
thistles and shamrock, in gold thread and beads. Made by Hook,
Knowles and Co Ltd, makers to the Royal Family.** *The London
Museum*

**65 Right: 1911 – Queen Mary's coronation dress, detail. The
fabric is white satin embroidered in a variety of gold threads. The
design by Jessie Robinson contains the thistle, rose, shamrocks
and oak leaves. The dress was made by Reville and Rossiter, the
Queen's dressmakers.** *The London Museum*

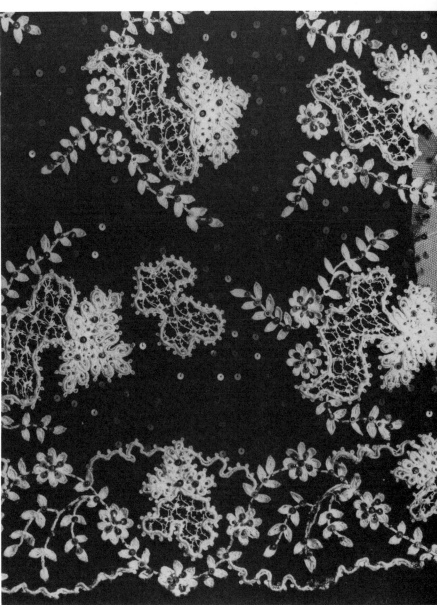

66 Left: 1912–1914. A dress in black net over black silk chiffon and lace, decorated with embroidery and worked on the Cornely machine. *The Costume Study Centre, Bath*

67 Above: 1912–1914. A detail from a dress in black net over black silk chiffon and lace. The embroidery is worked on the Cornely machine in cream cotton, giving the appearance of lace appliqué. The leaves, flowers and motifs are all embroidered; the cream motifs have corded edges. Small gunmetal sequins are scattered over the net while silver sequins and small silver beads decorate the flowers. Very small beads are sewn onto the 'lace' motifs, all by hand. *The Costume Study Centre, Bath*

68 1913. A panel by Emily Cannon. The panel is embroidered in a variety of colours, mainly in long and short stitch. The design was drawn by her, sent to the firm of Morris and Co to be painted onto the fabric, and then worked by her. The pomegranate panel was made for Helen Grundy's grandfather who studied Hebrew and the Bible as a hobby. The Hebrew script reads: 'As a place of pomegranates are thy temples within thy locks'.
Loaned by Helen Grundy

69 Above: 1915. A curtain of creamy yellow linen, worked in wools. The four repeating patterns have blue leaves in running and couching stitches and dull sage green leaves in chain stitch. The ovals are in salmon pink with brown surrounds. *The Embroiderers' Guild*

70 Right: 1915 – Doris Taylor. A small bag with a drawstring which was entered for the City and Guilds of London Institute Examinations. The bag is of cream satin, the hand-made drawstring in orange and cream silk, the tassels in grey-green buttonhole and cream silk. The embroidery is finely worked in silks, with light green stems in stem stitch enclosing small sprigs in pale turquoise fly stitch with yellow french knots. The flower petals are in cool blue to pale cream in long and short stitch, the ends in satin stitch and french knots. A narrow $\frac{2}{3}$ in. (3 mm) border is worked in yellow fly stitch, cream stem stitch and turquoise straight stitches. $8\frac{1}{2}$ in. (21 cm) square. *Loaned by Margaret Wimpenny*

71 Left: 1910–1920 – Doris Taylor. A large, unfinished panel illustrating the fairy tale of Thumblina, in appliqué and stitching. The background is a dark, natural linen with the kneeling figure in a cream silk dress, the outlines of drapery in long split stitch in cream and yellow. The cloak is cream brocade embroidered in bright blue and green floss silk in satin and split stitch, as is the decorated bodice. The hair is auburn in split stitch in silk, covered with a caul of green laid work and blue and green pattern. The skin of the child and the woman is applied in very pale pink silk. The figure is outlined in brown silk in split stitch. The attendants wear dull green-grey linen coats, the hat is a dull purple; stockings and waistcoats are cream, with embroidery in blue and green, and large yellow buttons couched in floss silk. Dull purple shoes, cream hair and pale pink flesh are all in linen appliqué. The flowers are in pink appliqué with long and short stitched edges in pinks and reds; the leaves are in long and short stitch in two shades of green with brown spines; the pots are grey. The lily is applied cream linen with off-white edges in long and short stitch and leaves in greens and its pot dull mauve. The water is in dull blues and pale greens in back stitch, the frog in shades of yellow. The roses are in pink linen with satin stitch worked from pale to dark mauve centres. The leaves are blue-green and lighter green in long and short and the stems are mauve and brown in long split stitch. The background trees are mauve and grey-green slanting satin stitch. *Loaned by Margaret Wimpenny*

72 Top Right: 1915. A banner for Sir Arthur Schuster, Professor of Chemistry, Manchester University, President of the Association, 1915. The designer and worker are unknown. The ground is black satin with applied fawn satin for the ground, blue for the sky. Trees, guns and the snake are all applied black satin. The figure is in a finely woven gold thread fabric with satin stitch and couched outlines in floss silk. The braid and cord are in gold metal threads. *The British Association for the Advancement of Science*

73 Right: 1916 – Eve Simmons. A child's smock in shantung with appliqué in scarlet linen and scarlet stitching. The dress is based on a rectangular pattern. *The Holborne Museum, Bath*

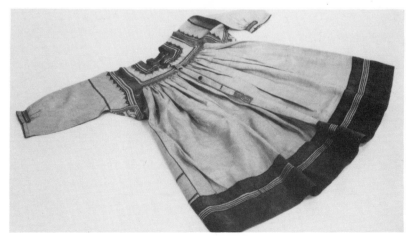

74 Far left: 1913 – Margaret Holden-Jones. A panel worked in silks on linen made for the winding sheets of mummies. The flowers are in white with apricot centres, and outlines in pinkish reds. The stems are a dull pinkish-red; the leaves are in greens with light brown stems while the strawberries are in red and dull mauve. Stitches used are eyelets for the leaves, brick stitch for the flowers, whipped stem and stem stitch. A heavily knotted silk fringe completes the panel. 9 in. × 22½ in. (23 cm × 57.5 cm).

75 Left: Pre-1920 (probably between 1916 and 1919) – Doris Taylor. Sampler on coarse natural linen, stitched in blue and pale natural threads, possibly worked with Grace Christie. A great variety of stitches is shown on the sampler. 6½ in. × 18¼ in (17 cm × 46.5 cm). *Loaned by Margaret Wimpenny*

76 Above: Early twentieth century. A table mat on dull blue green linen, worked in perle cotton, in pinks, greens, cream, yellow, grey blues and mauves. Stitches include buttonhole, herringbone, satin and stem stitch. About 20 in. (51 cm) square. *The Embroiderers' Guild*

77 Above: 1918 – Doris Taylor. A panel 'The Blue Bird', in blue and white threads on cream linen. The panel is in six episodes and each part contains stitches worked on the counted thread of the material. Darning, russian drawn ground, cross stitch and other canvas stitches with back stitch outlines, pulled stitches and hem stitching are used. Grace Christie shows this embroidery in her book *Samplers and Stitches*. 9 in. × 28¼ in. (23 cm × 72 cm). *Loaned by Margaret Wimpenny*

78 Above: Pre-1920 – Grace Christie. A panel or sampler worked on cream linen in cream threads, showing a number of composite stitches and others. Among these are sheaf, German interlacing, raised stem band, russian drawn ground, eyelets, pekinese and hem stitching. This panel was worked for Grace Christie's book *Samplers and Stitches*, published in 1920. *Victoria and Albert Museum, London*

79 Right: 1913–1918 – Doris Taylor. A small panel of Jeanne D'Arc is worked on a very fine, natural linen. The embroidery completely conceals the background, which is in underside couching in fine gold thread; the foreground is in horizontal lines of grey floss silk, covered with stems in green silk and forget-me-knots in satin stitch. The border is couched, untwisted grey silk, in a darker grey, edged with green floss silk couched in a zig-zag stitch. St Joan wears a garment of cream silk stitched in underside couching. The cloak, in various reds, is in long and short stitch. The armour is in a variety of grey threads in untwisted floss silk in long and short stitch. Features are in split stitch following the contours of the bones. The hair is in the same stitch in dark orange silk, while the halo is in fine Japanese gold couched in blue silk with blue jewels. The sword is in fawn split stitch with a red jewel made by the artist, in enamel. The underdress is in blue and yellow laid silk. *Loaned by Margaret Wimpenny*

80 Above: Probably 1916–1918 – Doris Taylor. A sampler on coarse, dark, natural linen, showing a variety of counted thread patterns. The 'Fox and Grapes', 11 in. × 10 in. (28 cm × 26 cm) is in mauve silk and green silk with rust fruits. The 'Owl in the Tree', 11 in. × 9¾ in. (28 cm × 25 cm) is in similar colours, again showing a variety of patterns. The outlines are in whipped stem stitch and the fabrics are joined with knotted herringbone. Lines of hem stitch frame the panels which are 15¼ in. (39 cm) wide including the frame. *Loaned by Margaret Wimpenny*

The Twenties

At the beginning of the 1920s materials were in short supply for embroidery, and pre-War ideas were revived. As the decade advanced changes were noticeable, although the peasant trend continued with the 'tea shoppe' smocks embroidered in wools or silks on linen. At the Royal College of Art dresses often remained long and full skirted, sometimes embroidered, although by the middle of the decade, fashion dictated skirts above the knees, lengthening again by the 1930s.

The decade saw the rise of film stars, the introduction of rayon for clothes, the expansion of *haute-couture* in Paris, with model gowns lavishly decorated with embroidery, and metal threads and beads a favourite means of embellishment in the early twenties.

Dress in the early twenties

In Paris Lanvin showed a collection of Aztec embroideries in which brilliant colours were used. Beads were very much in evidence for fringes or for more solid areas of pattern, or they were combined with sequins and machine embroidery. Peasant styles were also fashionable in France as well as in England. According to Georgina Howell in *Vogue* 'bright Balkan embroidery' decorated Chanel's black crêpe-de-chine garments and appliqué of crimson and scarlet poppies on black, or black on white or vice-versa, with bold simple shapes, enhanced skirts or tunics, sometimes covering them.

In Great Britain model gowns of chiffon or silk georgette were decorated with appliqué, with metal thread and silk stitchery or sometimes were partly or entirely covered in beads or sequins or a combination of both (pages 109, 110). The Persian garden, landscape and geometric patterns were favourites. Embroidery on costume, both for day and evening wear, continued in fashion during the early twenties (pages 101, 103, 105, 112, 113, 114). In 1923 beaded and jewelled embroidered garments and accessories were reminiscent of pre-War times.

It seems that numerous ideas developed from current events and in 1922 with the discovery of Tutankhamen's tomb, embroideries based on Egyptian designs appeared in Paris and in London. An advertisement for a blouse in a London shop said 'New, original designs can be had in all white, white embroidered black, navy and Egyptian colours. The design is an exact reproduction of the hieroglyphics of the King, from the tomb of Luxor'. The illustration shows the hieroglyphics surrounded by naturalistic flowers in the twenties style. Hieroglyphic embroidery had a short-lived popularity as did Egyptian-style jewellery.

Fine silk net was embroidered with darning patterns in silk threads during the early twenties. Floral forms were superseded by geometric ones, stripes, zigzags and squares. This means of decoration was fashionable for garments as also was darning in silk or artificial silk thread on square filet net. It was popular too to darn solidly into the square mesh cotton dishcloth, joining two together to make a sleeveless 'jumper', and this darning became a craze, with women's magazines giving instructions and charts for building up geometric designs. Complete garments were made quite cheaply by this means. (Page 104.)

Mr Reville, one of the Queen's dressmakers, writing in 1923 of dress after the War, said that ornament rather than severity was popular, but could be overdone and embroidery was now seen on day and evening gowns and even fur was decorated. He gave good advice: '. . . the dress designer as well as the embroiderer should always have in mind the character of the gown and the occasion on which it is to be worn . . . there must be some connection between the ornament and the fabric'. Queen Mary's coronation robes and other garments worn by Her Majesty were examples of those with decoration 'planned and executed with an eye to the requirements of the occasion.' He said: 'Never in the whole field of feminine dress has embroidery been so beautiful and varied, and fashion sanctioned its use to so great an extent as today . . . taste and judgment is essential if embroidery is not to be overdone. . . . Think of what can be used, rococo flowers, embroidery in chenille, embroidery in flat silks, embroidery in wool that suggests a rich pile carpet. Beads of every sort and kind, of every shape and size. Paillettes, jet, gold thread, silver thread, tinsel and other metallics'. What a profusion of ideas must have developed from all these ingredients. (Article in *Embroidery*).

Machine embroidery

Machine embroidery was fashionable, carried out on the Schiffli machine, with its multiple needles that could work a number of identical patterns by the pantograph method (see page 114); or on the Cornely machine that could be set for chain stitch, mossing or braiding. Metal thread was often used for machine embroidery worked on the trade machines.

Instruction in the use of trade embroidery machines, both the Irish and the Cornely, was given in the London Technical and Trade Institutes and others in the 1920s, a great deal of technically excellent work being produced as machine embroidery became more in demand in the trade. An article on machine embroidery in *The Embroideress* described the trade machines and also said 'the designer for embroidery to be carried out on the machine, must realise what can be done and what should be avoided. For instance, it is seldom advisable to copy on the machine a design originally prepared for handwork'. Another article in 1923 said 'the embroidery machine, like the sewing machine, has come to stay'.

The Bauhaus

At this time too, new ideas on art, craft and industry were being formulated in Germany and one of the major influences to have far reaching effects on design in Europe was The Bauhaus which opened in Weimar in 1919 under the direction of Walter Gropius, an architect of some standing. In 1926 the school moved to Dessau and flourished until its closure by Hitler in 1933. Its aim was to link together commercial art and fine art and to produce designers of distinction, in other words to fuse art and industry. The school produced in the Germany of the late 1920s and the early 1930s designs which influenced other European countries, particularly the Nordic ones. These countries in their turn influenced English design and consequently the embroidery of the thirties. Embroidery also flourished in Germany at this time. Anni Albers taught weaving and carried out embroidery at The Bauhaus; her husband, Josef Albers, lectured on colour theory and a number of excellent painters taught design, including Paul Klee and Moholy-Nagy.

Exhibitions with influence

Artists such as Picasso, Braque and Juan Gris, among others, had been exploring cubism for some time and their styles were beginning to influence design before the twenties. Another source of design which led to the styles of the twenties and thirties in architecture and industrial design was derived from old American-Indian cultures, particularly those of Mexico, which were seen with adaptations in the Paris Exhibition of 1925 – L'Exposition Internationale des Arts Decoratifs et Industriels Modernes. This exhibition displayed applied arts on an international scale, where completely new ideas and styles were noticeable which were to culminate in the severe, geometric designs of the thirties. Sonia Delauney's patchwork garments made a strong impact and really stamped out the copying of traditional embroideries so prevalent during the early part of the twentieth century and even after the War in England. This exhibition had far-reaching effects and together with the interest in American-Indian art helped in the evolution of the geometric designs and the clear-cut forms and patterns as a counteraction against the ornateness of the Russian Ballet which had previously influenced colour and style. (Page 116.)

At the end of the decade, votes for women over 21 were sanctioned. There were new movements in painting, experiments were being made in the German theatre and in German films. Photography was a developing art, with Cecil Beaton as an exponent of this medium. The wireless was becoming popular and in spite of growing economic difficulties, the arts flourished.

Crafts revival

The revival of interest in the crafts, including embroidery, after the War led to the first school of embroidery being held in 1920 in the Victoria and Albert Museum. Another one was held in 1922, conducted by Joan Drew, for those teaching in village institutes. These schools were the outcome of the book *Educational Needlecraft* published in 1911, already mentioned.

In Glasgow too *An Embroidery Book* published in 1920 by A and C Black, was written by Ann Knox-Arthur, who was teaching at the Glasgow School of Art, and took Ann Macbeth's place when she retired. This had an interesting foreword by Ann Macbeth, in which she said:

'To be in a healthy and living state, our art should be constantly changing its fashion; if it stands still, it is retrograde . . . changes it has undergone are due almost entirely to the manufacture of printed patterns. . . . The British needlewoman follows blindly where the merchant leads, and British design for needlework is almost a dead thing. . . . The commonest failing of the designers of this country is that they think that beauty lies in the elaboration of ornament.'

The Embroiderers' Guild

The Society of Certificated Embroideresses after a General Meeting in 1920, changed its name to the Embroiderers' Guild, with a constitution devised by Mary Antrobus and Louisa Preece. The Guild now became a flourishing concern, a lending library was formed and portfolios showing the use of stitches were assembled for reference.

As mentioned already, Louisa Pesel became the first President. The first Annual Report was printed in 1923. Membership required the submission of three different types of work to 12 judges, approved by the Authorities of the Victoria and Albert Museum. Queen Mary was a Patron from 1925 to 1953, the Worshipful Company of Broderers Vice-Patrons in 1928.

The first public exhibition of the Embroiderers' Guild was held in November 1923, when embroideries from other countries were shown. The Wiener Werkstatte Modern School of Austria exhibited exciting work. Designs by well-known English artists such as Duncan Grant, Paul Nash and Roger Fry were mentioned, often worked by other artists who were embroiderers in their own right. Among those who exhibited were Madeleine Clifton, Grace Christie, Joan Drew and Marian Stoll. A good standard was produced. Adaptations from historical pieces were submitted by the Royal School of Needlework. This exhibition with its examples of continental work, particularly that from the Wiener Werkstatte School of lace and embroidery whose design was in advance of that in Britain, may have inspired Rebecca Crompton.

Societies

In 1921 the Modern Embroidery Society in Edinburgh was formed by eight embroiderers, the aim being to hold annual exhibitions and to invite people outside the group to show work. In this way the society hoped to keep in touch with other crafts and designers. It was noted that the members were all designers as well as embroiderers which accounted for the good drawing and colour and the varied character of the work on show. At the first exhibition Helen Gorrie, Dorothy Angus and Louisa Chart exhibited and Louisa Pesel sent work from England.

The British Institute of Industrial Art, formed in 1920, two years later staged an exhibition at the Victoria and Albert Museum called 'British Craftsmanship', where, according to a report in the *Illustrated London News* of February 1922, 'Art and Industry mingle in beautiful craftsmanship, useful and satisfactory'. The account continued with a description of 'The Blue Bird' by Doris Taylor (page 86), saying 'Mrs Christie and her pupils illustrate the beauty of stitching stories and fancies in delicate colours into samplers, needlebooks, mats and even brooches. The story of The Blue Bird is unfolded with a clever needle, working in a single colour with a restrained and pleasing design. Mrs Christie's animal samplers are particularly beautiful examples'. At this exhibition Margaret Holden-Jones's brooches were shown (page 111).

Schools of art

In schools of art the freedom to experiment was increasing; original design from non-historical sources was encouraged, although fine silk embroidery on silk or linen was still popular. Larger pieces of work were attempted, such as wall hangings or portières which became popular and led to a broader outlook on embroidery. These were worked on coarser fabrics such as crash, a mixture of linen and cotton being popular, with its warp and weft of different tones of fawn.

Birmingham School of Art

Embroiderers working during the 1920s are not well documented but several were doing excellent work in teaching. **Isabel Catterson-Smith** in the Birmingham School of Art advocated the working of stitchery straight on to the material, embroidering ideas based on plants. The use of brightly coloured wools stitched on white or coloured linens was encouraged. She felt the need for pupils to learn stitches and to think out their own ways in which to apply them. Eleven to 15 year-old children attended the branch schools in Birmingham where they used pictorial subjects for self-expression; they also embroidered household articles and accessories, the craft being taught in order to develop the imagination. Young students were given suggestions for ideas but advanced students set their own projects.

Bournville School of Art

An example of a very flourishing school in which embroidery played a prominent part from its inception was the Bournville School of Art, Birmingham, housed in Ruskin Hall, which was built in 1903 as a social centre for the developing Bournville Estate. Ruskin Hall became a school of crafts and in 1910 drawing and painting were introduced too. The school flourished under two authorities, the Birmingham Education Authority and the Bournville Village Trust. The classes were always filled and the school expanded, with extensions built in 1927 to 1928 and later. Ages ranged from 15 to 70 years of age. Embroidery was introduced early into the school curriculum, obtaining an excellent reputation, the approach in teaching being one of liveliness and experiment, with freedom for a student to develop her own ideas.

Edinburgh College of Art

In the Edinburgh College of Art embroidery flourished in the early twenties under Louisa Chart. The College had its own diploma and all students took a general course before the advanced one, in which they specialised in their chosen fields. Embroidery classes were held in the Applied Art Department, where plant form, design and historical ornament were studied. The students commenced with linen samplers, using coloured wools and silks, the designs being built up with stitches as the work progressed. Advice on colour choice was given when necessary. Free choice of work and technique were encouraged, the students evolving their own way of developing the embroidery. Some drew careful designs on paper, others worked straightaway on the fabric. The construction of articles was taught too, and classes often contained 30 to 40 students. The copying of historical work was discouraged, although it was used as a source of inspiration.

Embroiderers and designers in the twenties

An artist working during the twenties about whom very little is known personally was **Marian Stoll**, apparently an outstanding embroiderer, producing exciting and individual work which was appreciated in Germany but seems to have been too 'avant garde' for England. She said that it took her years to unlearn her training in America and that she couldn't draw naturalistically, so drew as she felt. She worked often from very small watercolour sketches, translating these into large embroideries in coloured wools. From information known about her and her work she was a strong character and an artist with great individuality who went her own way. Several exhibitions of her work in Oxford were reviewed between 1924 and 1926, in the German magazine devoted to embroidery and lace, *Stickereien und Spitzen.* From photographs of her work it is interesting to trace her development, from the more ordinary examples to the very strong personal work of the later exhibitions (page 157). The earlier German magazines show examples of a ballet dancer in pulled stitches, a tray cloth, a blouse and a panel of a tree with a summerhouse. More typical of the later styles was a panel of a summerhouse, surrounded by swirling clouds in a circular conformation, the stitchery completely obscuring the fabric.

In the 1926 edition of Lewis F Day's book *Art and Needlework* an illustration of Marian Stoll's 'Ballet Dancer' was included, the description saying' The muslin ground has the pattern stitched in a tiny buttonhole . . . superimposed after the ground was done. The grounds are pulled fabric stitches invented on the spur of the moment, to form the shapes the worker desired. It is original work of a very high order'. A later exhibition in 1925 contained a panel of a garden with a figure and a house, again in solid stitching, and a still life of a pot with a plant, overlaid with shafts of light worked in chain stitch and couching, also covering the ground fabric. She used mainly couching, satin and long and short stitches for these embroideries that covered the fabric entirely. At this exhibition, held in November-December 1925 in the Oxford Arts Club, she gave a talk, saying: 'The idea is the thing, the stitches will come to order when required . . . three stitches are sufficient . . . satin, split, couching . . . an artist has the right to express any mood, to take advantage of any emotion, however painful or transitory'.

A critic said of Marian Stoll's exhibition in Oxford 'all one's preconceived ideas about the purpose and function of needlework and all reflections on traditional embroidery took flight in the first glance around this amazing exhibition'. She was considered by the more advanced embroiderers to be the finest designer and embroiderer of her time. She said: 'Things should be produced from the inner consciousness . . . be free with not too much study in museums . . . as one is frightened by the masterpiece or could be accused of copying'.

Marian Stoll was very keen on modern work. She strongly condemned the poor quality of design in the twenties and said 'why do people appreciate the modern approach to all crafts, except embroidery?'. She was scathing about those who stayed in the 'Jacobean' tradition:

'Every English embroiderer who continues to copy or to adapt old work is doing her lot to debase the standard of English embroidery . . . which is mortifyingly low compared with the average product in numerous European countries, where only good modern design is accepted for public exhibition . . . on the continent design is excellent, execution occasionally defective. Here . . . the execution leaves little to be desired . . . but alas . . . designs are Jacobean, Elizabethan, Victorian. If an attempt at modernity is made this usually ends in a bunch of cherries or forget-me-nots . . . all carefully drawn from nature with a capital N!'.

This article shocked people as it was meant to, some people agreeing, others strongly against it. Many misinterpreted her message, which was to move with the times, thinking that she implied that old work was not to be copied as it was poor.

She wrote other articles, all of which tried to arouse people. In fact she was a marvellous catalyst, but no-one seems to have recollections of her or her work.

Another artist who promoted embroidery and by her criticisms helped to raise the standard of design was **Mary Hogarth**, an excellent painter and artist and a good draughtswoman of architectural subjects. She was friendly with the Bloomsbury Group and although she became an embroiderer in her own right she often carried out the designs of others; among these artists were Duncan Grant (page 120) and William Tryon who produced many designs for chair seats, cushion covers and hangings. Much of this embroidery was in canvas stitches or in darning which covered the ground entirely. She sometimes worked on fabric woven from handspun threads, thus giving a more interesting textural surface than the regularity of machine made canvas. In 1921 she became the Honorary Secretary of the Embroiderers' Guild and in 1922 the Honorary Treasurer. She was a member of the council and the panel of judges and wrote some excellent criticisms of exhibitions held by the Guild. Joan Lodge, a student, found Mary Hogarth a person of tremendous character who was always working. She said 'she urged me to work, as I had a rather bad habit of standing and staring'. She remembered a remark made by Mary Hogarth about a piece of white embroidery, worked by a student at the Royal School of Needlework, saying that she thought that the technique was too good. (Colour plate 5.)

In a review of the first exhibition held by the Embroiderers' Guild in May 1922 as a semi-private affair, Mary Hogarth said 'Embroidery is only alive when it expresses what the present is thinking. We are apt to lose ourselves in a multitude of stitches, forgetting that they are only a means to an end. Someone invented each stitch . . . as a means of expression, why should we not invent a new stitch . . . to express what we have to say?' The one example of Cornely machine embroidery received the comment 'Are we to use machines?'.

In 1922 *The Embroideress* was published by Pearsall and Company. This magazine contained articles of general interest, on historical embroideries and on those from different countries, on techniques and specialized subjects. Reviews of exhibitions and new books on embroidery were included.

There seemed to be several categories of work being produced at this time, in which the aims were different. One category relied on correctness of stitchery, with design a secondary consideration, another emphasised the importance of the design with stitchery to interpret the idea of lesser importance, where the methods by which results were achieved could be varied as long as the design was strong. Another type again enjoyed the monotony of repetition such as cross stitch or tent stitch on canvas, or pulled work on linen.

A variety of magazines on embroidery and other 'women's' subjects was published; some were good, some poor, but their common aim was to promote the crafts. Transfers were issued by some of these magazines, for embroidery on lingerie: broderie anglaise, net work, net insets embroidered with darning and satin stitches were among the techniques suggested.

A complaint in one magazine on the transfers of the times was that 'There is a terrible dearth of good design available in the form of transfers'. The bowl of circular flowers was much favoured but the most popular of all transfers was the ubiquitous crinoline lady with a bonnet but without a face, embroidered on all manner of articles for the household (page 146).

The Embroiderers' Guild in 1923 bought up a stock of transfers belonging to a private firm and from then onwards made their own collection of designs based on museum study. The idea was to encourage those who did not want to carry out designs themselves.

European trends

Mary Hogarth taught weekly classes for the Embroiderers' Guild in 1923; she also reviewed exhibitions held in Europe. One of these, in France, impressed her as it did many people. It was by a Mlle Monnier, who in 1924 held an exhibition for which she had embroidered panels with the background of the fabric covered with stitching, used solely to express what she had to say in illustrating poems. In fact it was said that 'she has not allowed herself to become the slave of stitches'. Mary

Hogarth, in describing trends in Europe at this time, said the emphasis was on the expression of literary ideas rather than towards pure decoration. She did not agree with stitching completely covering the fabric, nor that it should be framed like a picture. She said 'a little crumpling up, some folds do give more play of light on the material used, do enable us to see the manner in which the result has been arrived at [sic]' and suggested that these were part of the limitations of embroidery. Marian Stoll, whose work has been described, covered her backgrounds.

Kathleen Whyte, a student at Grays School of Art, Aberdeen said that she carried out some very large embroideries, the designs being drawn as charcoal cartoons under the tuition of James Hamilton, head of the design department. The stitchery was worked in the embroidery department with Dorothy Angus. Household articles, cushion covers, tray cloths and tablecloths, fire screens and tea cosies, however, remained favourite articles for decoration in many schools, together with articles of dress, such as small bags, jackets for occasional wear, scarves and hat bands, worked finely in silk threads, on silk, wool or linen.

Dress in the mid-twenties

Apart from the trained artists who were designing and carrying out embroideries of a high standard, a great deal of work was produced by those with little or no artistic training, some making their own less sophisticated patterns, others using transfers. Lingerie was often hand embroidered, made in crêpe-de-chine, silk georgette, cotton lawn and other fine fabrics, worked in silk threads, usually in self colour. The human figure in miniature, clothed or unclothed, was popular for design, as were small satin stitched flowers like forget-me-nots and roses tightly worked in bullion and french knots. Many designs were stitched in outline only, in fine, slightly raised whip stitch; small leaves were worked in padded satin stitch; eyelets, cutwork and insets of darned net were all means of decorating lingerie during this decade.

In Paris the embroidered garment for day wear tended to disappear in the mid-twenties although some designers continued to decorate evening gowns, and beads were seen on the floating panels of knitted rayon afternoon wear in England. Appliqué of satin and net in the form of large floral motifs, somewhat stylized, decorated the low-waisted bodices of garments in silk chiffon or georgette. Appliqué was perhaps one of the simplest ways by which to add interest without too much intricate stitchery, with sequins, diamanté and metal threads often an extra embellishment. (Page 120.)

Design

Geometric patterns sustained popularity, the circle in various sizes representing floral forms (page 148). If these shapes were applied, the edges of the fabric were covered with blanket stitch or buttonhole stitch. Sometimes the edges were turned under and slip stitched as blind appliqué. Sometimes the circles were worked solidly in buttonhole stitch, in brightly coloured wools, on crash or linen, in a series of overlapping and concentric circles in different sizes. Foliage, when included, was represented by oval shapes worked in blanket stitch, following the contours, round and round. Bunches of flowers and leaves, bowls of flowers or fruit were also carried out in appliqué, often using linen or cotton, on the crash which was a popular fabric during the twenties. Surface stitching of designs reminiscent of the seventeenth-century Jacobean styles were favourites, carried out in brightly coloured, soft wools that faded quickly. The so-called 'Jacobean' fire screen worked on commercially stamped fabric was much in evidence too, embroidered in crewel wools, or even in stranded cottons. Cushion covers, table runners and chair backs were popular articles for decoration. Embroidered garments were worked in silk or cotton threads, or sometimes in linen thread on linen while the smock, usually in coloured linen or cotton, was often decorated in several different colours of thread. Many of these styles remained in fashion well into the thirties, as did traditional embroidery, although more original work was appearing in exhibitions. The imitation of painting, with shading to give reality, was decreasing. Flat pattern, omitting embroidered outlines which had been fashionable earlier in the century, developed as blind appliqué. Appliqué of simple shapes stitched with contrasting colours in blanket stitch or buttonhole over the edges was typical of hand embroidery by the non-art trained embroiderer in the late twenties, but a change was taking place in the world of art, with experiments in styles and media. Embroidery was less affected than other arts such as painting and sculpture, in which the exciting developments on the continent – Cubism, Futurism and Dadaism – had strong impact; but the craft in England was perhaps influenced by such places as the Royal College of Art and the Central School of Arts and Crafts as well as by the numerous schools of art both in London and in the provinces, where embroidery was included as a part of the training.

The Royal College of Art

Under Kathleen Harris's guidance at the Royal College, students were encouraged to go out and to draw from reality, to experiment and to try out new ideas. These students often became the teachers of the thirties and forties; some of them revolutionised attitudes to embroidery in the schools of art and in other educational establishments. This was necessary as in the mid-twenties design on paper in the schools of art consisted often of the filling in of given shapes, such as the diamond, the lunette or the ogee, with plant and other forms, basing the patterns on such flowers as the daffodil, the tulip or the dog rose, carefully stylized and planned, with foliage to fit into the appropriate confines. Geometric patterns were treated in a similar way. This was known as space filling and was the only general design carried out, although for specific crafts such as embroidery, these designs were modified or patterns were devised to fit the shapes to be worked.

Independent Gallery Exhibition

A new outlook was seen in October 1925 in 'an exhibition from new designs' at the Independent Gallery, in London, with designs by Duncan Grant, Roger Fry, Vanessa Bell and William Tryon, worked in cross stitch by women artists, but showing power in the results. The embroidery was worked in wools, mainly for upholstery such as chair seats and stool tops, with one carpet and a striking cushion cover designed by William Tryon and worked by Mary Hogarth. Landscapes were favourite subjects, with excellent colour and individuality. Mary Rolleston, the editor of *The Embroideress* said: 'it is certain that a new note has been struck in the history of needlework'. She also said at the same time: 'Until they [the students] realise that the three things – colour, design, stitching – are interdependent, our national embroidery will never be something that we can really be proud of'. During this year the Society of Women Artists accepted embroidery in their exhibition and although they had little space available, this was a step in recognising embroidery as a serious art.

Elsie Grant ARCA writing on modern embroidery mentioned prominent embroiderers of the twenties and well known artists who were designing for embroidery, such as Duncan Grant the painter (page 120), and **Claude Flight**, a print maker who executed machine embroidery with appliqué, carrying out the work himself. He also designed for hand embroidery which was worked by embroiderers with good techniques, one being a Marjorie Lawrence who carried out much of the work. It was said that his design and colour were more important than the stitchery, and that most of his designs could have been worked as effectively by machine as by hand. They were mainly geometric, abstract and carefully planned within the shapes to be filled.

New schools of design in northern Europe and in central Europe were set up in the mid-twenties, encouraged by the Paris Exhibition of 1925. The wish to create rather than to copy had arrived; most art schools taught embroidery, although accounts of individual schools suggested that exhibitions of work varied in standard; such as 'many kinds of work were shown, all excellent, with strong, fresh colour' or 'work was very uneven . . . with the use of unsuitable materials and a lack of originality'. Most craft exhibitions showed embroidery, some of which was original in concept while some was a translation of painting and historical examples.

In 1926 an exhibition at Burlington House by the Arts and Crafts Exhibition Society contained embroidery where canvas work, pictorial hangings and garments were juxtaposed. The criticism of this exhibition was that much of the work was laboured, of a poor standard, with a lack of vitality, although well known embroiderers were represented.

Books

Batsford published at this time *Simple Stitch Patterns for Embroidery* by Ann Brandon Jones, written with the aim of learning to build up original designs from a geometric basis, with well-known stitches to determine the character of the pattern. This was done without drawing and as ready-made transfers were now condemned by educational authorities, this means of pattern making became popular. Books such as *Embroidery and Design in the New Stitchery* and *Constructive and Decorative Stitchery*, published in 1926 by Pitman and first written by Elizabeth Foster in 1921, were appearing as re-issues and as an aid to teachers in schools. The Educational Needlecraft Association had opened in London in Deptford in 1918; the New Needlecraft which was originally inspired by the book by Ann Macbeth and Margaret Swanson was developed by this association. For children under 11 the old and boring needlework classes were giving way to the use of simple stitches and colour with which to build up pattern and to decorate garments. Elizabeth Foster said that 'simplicity in design, material and workmanship is the keynote of the new method' and 'the New Needlework does away with the need of machine printed embroideries'; ie those with transfer patterns stamped on to the materials. Lewis F Day added a chapter in 1926 to his book published originally in 1900 *Art and Needlework* on 'Modern Developments'. He says 'we ought to try to decide whether any of it has risen to the level of an art'. He advocates building up patterns by the counted thread method in the beginning and that drawing of form is 'best taught . . . by the use of the point. . . . We should not be afraid to express the present age' and 'to make one medium try to do what another medium does better, is to vulgarise the work, however well executed'. He was aware of the development of embroidery on the continent, saying 'in central Europe . . . a real art of embroidery is being brought into being. It strikes a new note in design. . . . It has a gossamer like quality not seen previously. It has a combination of lines and spaces'.

Lack of standards in embroidery

Except for the few artists practising the craft and the work produced by students in the schools of art, it would seem from reviews in the 1920s that embroidery was far behind other crafts in ideas and in design, with the emphasis still on technical achievement rather than on ideas. The really good embroiderers who were also artists appeared to have scorned the exhibitions by so called 'amateurs'. The standard of many shows therefore remained low, as those exhibiting were often unaware of current trends in art. They did not appreciate the work of the good designers, so were unable to keep abreast of the times or to produce lively work of a contemporary style.

An exhibition held in 1927 by the Embroiderers' Guild at the Walker Galleries in London was criticised by Mary Hogarth as '. . . being thin on quality, although there were some good hangings by R Willis and E. Eraut, both students at the RCA'. In comparison with the work of well-known textile designers such as Enid Marx and Phyllis Barron, whose prints were hand blocked or painted, or with designs by painters such as Paul Nash, and styles expressing ideas of the day in batik, embroidery was considerably behind in outlook. This was due to the fact that with a few exceptions, the craft was not in the hands of artists. She continued:

'Embroiderers making direct copies of works of art of the past, or taking designs of the past without understanding them . . . making travesties of them, or what is worse . . . making feeble designs that have no leading lines or spaces, without aesthetic idea . . . have no realisation that the colour must form pattern as well as the lines and spaces, and that stitches must also form pattern. Good stitching, just the actual technique can never make up for the

1   1890—William Morris. Tulip panel 48 in. x 22 in. (122 cm x 55.8 cm). Worked in thick silks by May Morris. The whole concept is bold and full of vitality. *Embroiderers' Guild*

2 1909—K Maud Mills. Peacock panel in the late
Art Nouveau style. Velvets and silks applied to the
blue silk background. *Victoria and Albert Museum,
London*

3   1912—Joan Drew. 'Castle on Cliff'. *Given by
Blackheath Hall and now belonging to the
Embroiderers' Guild*

4 1918. Detail from an altar frontal in a church in Thaxted, Essex. *Photograph: Nancy Kimmins*

5 1920s — Mary Hogarth. Partly worked panel. Darning and other stitches in silks on linen. *Loaned by Joan Lodge*

6   About 1920. A circular panel on linen worked in silks in a variety of stitches including stem, buttonhole and chain. Lettering was popular at this time, often incorporated with floral decoration. *Victoria and Albert Museum, London*

7   Early twentieth century—Grace Christie. Part of a panel worked in silks on linen in a variety of stitches. This panel is typical of her embroidery as she would draw meticulous details of butterflies, birds and plants before using them in her design

8   1930—Aileen Molly Booker. 'The South of France'. The background is covered entirely with wools worked in stem stitch in different directions

9

9   1932—Elizabeth Grace Thomson. 'My Mother'.
A panel approximately 20 in. x 27 in. (50.8 cm x
68.5 cm) exhibited at the Victoria and Albert Museum
in 1932. The embroidery is on linen, worked in a
variety of threads and stitches, including pulled work
and couching

absence of these essential qualities that go to make a work of art. Notable exceptions . . . come naturally from the work designed by the well known names . . . Fry, Grant, Bell and Nash'.

It was observed that there was good, original work shown by young, little known exhibitors, with small pictures on canvas that did not invade the realm of painting, and fewer copies of the past were exhibited.

In this year, however, the Modern Embroidery Society in Edinburgh held an exhibition where the standard of design and technique was the best so far seen. Louisa Chart lectured on stitches and their uses, and it was stressed that sound design was the criterion necessary before accepting work for exhibition. This concept led to enquiries from needlewomen for trained designers to instruct them. Dorothy Angus showed 'clever' work with a sense of humour: a screen and one of the best pieces in the exhibition 'Lucy Locket' in running and darning stitches. Other exhibitors were Helen Gorrie, Marian Stoll and Ethel Mairet, a weaver.

Trade schools examinations

The Clapham Trade School for Girls was opened now as an evening institute, but in 1931 became a day school for full-time instruction where embroidery was taught. The City and Guilds of London Institute examination syllabus in embroidery was revised during 1927–8, being divided into two parts: Part 1 Hand embroidery, with two grades, and Part 2 Machine embroidery with one grade. A separate drawing test of three hours provided a design with the main lines indicated which had to be completed and coloured; a simple design showing appropriate stitches was also required as a part of the test. In machine embroidery there was a three hour written paper, including the completion of a design. Practical work on the Cornely machine and the submission of class work or of work carried out in the trade workroom from the previous year was a part of the examination. Dress decoration and upholstery decoration had alternative questions.

Although she had no education in embroidery, **Mary Thomas** must be mentioned in the context of the late 1920s as in 1927 she became the editor of *The Needlewoman* magazine. She did a considerable amount of research in museums, had travelled widely and was very well read and already had experience on several magazines. She retained the position of editor very successfully until 1936 when she left to write more books, her first one, *Mary Thomas's Dictionary of Embroidery Stitches* having been published in 1934. This book was written as a result of requests sent to the magazine's service bureau asking about stitches. A great amount of confusion was caused by the various names given to one stitch. In order to clear up some of the difficulties, she devised the dictionary. This was extremely successful and a number of books followed, all receiving excellent reviews.

She frequently visited the Royal School of Needlework during the thirties and was in touch with current trends and ideas. She wrote four more books between 1936 and 1943 and if the Second World War had not intervened, she had planned to write a book on crochet to follow that on knitting patterns. Unfortunately she died soon after the War.

Several young students at the Royal College of Art were beginning to exhibit embroidery in 1927. One of them, **Rosamund Willis**, was an innovator and started a trend, with Mildred Lockyer, for making large hangings rather than the smaller works then in vogue. She designed and worked a number of embroideries in the late 1920s and early 1930s, which were shown at important exhibitions. She exploited the weave of the materials as a basis of her techniques, often darning the entire surface with a variety of patterns, sometimes using canvas stitches and darning together, sometimes working with appliqué and surface stitching. Her ideas were developed to a great extent from her environment, landscape and buildings being favourite subjects. She was fascinated by trees which were a feature of her watercolour paintings and later seen in embroideries. She attended Kathleen Harris's classes only when she required technical advice but all students were free to experiment, so she and Mildred Lockyer, a potter, tried out their ideas on a different scale. The 'Sheep in a Field' (see page 118) was worked at this time as was 'The Goose Girl' (page 145) which was a pastiche on a drawing of Frank Barber, a brilliant artist teaching at the Wimbledon School of Art. Rosamund Willis saw the drawing when visiting Mary Hogarth's studio and obtained permission to use it as a basis of her embroidery.

Rosamund Willis wrote an article for *Vogue* in 1928, on the embroidered panel which 'is said to be again in fashion', but she thought that few artists had seriously thought about embroidery for walls. She said that 'an embroidered panel should contain information or expression of fact, it should not fail to interest . . . it is to be looked at not once but many times'.

Design ideas had developed considerably in schools of art since the mid-twenties, with a wider choice of subject matter and more freedom for the students to pursue individual inclinations. Animals and birds, landscape and buildings as well as exotic plant forms were now a basis of design for embroidery. Canvas work became freer, sometimes employing a number of different stitches, and a wider range of embroidery techniques was introduced, although appliqué, darning on linen, surface stitchery and quilting remained in favour.

In 1928 the Arts and Crafts Exhibition Society show was praised for its printed and woven textiles, although the embroidery was very disappointing, as few examples contained 'ideas expressing the spirit of the times in which we live'. The exhibition by the Modern Embroidery Society in Edinburgh at this time appears to have been excellent with work by Ethel Mairet, Mabel Dawson, Joan Drew and Helen Gorrie. Dorothy Angus lectured on modern embroidery.

The Worshipful Company of Broderers in 1929 initiated an annual scholarship of ten guineas, for members of the Embroiderers' Guild who were less than 25 years of age. This continued until 1940.

At this time, 1929, I was a student at the Northampton School of Art studying embroidery for the Industrial Design examination. I was lucky, as a very lively teacher, Dorothy Thornton, arrived from the Royal College of Art before my training in this subject was concluded. My ideas completely changed as I had found the whole outlook on embroidery very boring before her arrival. Now I began to see possibilities in the craft. Having already worked small, neat flowers and leaves in silk threads on a fawn silk jacket which I hated, I now started work on a large curtain of bright blue hessian with a very wide border of circles each 12 in. (30 cm) in diameter outlined in thick black and white wools enclosing applied geometric four-petalled flowers, alternating in orange and white hessian. The curtain was embroidered entirely in black and white and hung in the school. It was the first piece of work that I found interesting to execute. This led to the designing of a fire screen of a tiger in a jungle where the imagination could run wild, and was worked on canvas by my mother in cross stitch only. In 1930 I took the examination and passed. It was theoretical, with the design questions worked out on paper.

The examiner was **Rebecca Crompton**, who had already gained a reputation as a teacher of dress design and embroidery in the Croydon School of Art where the work of her students was highly praised. The secretary of the Northampton School of Art remembers that as a young girl in the early twenties she was very struck by Rebecca Crompton's clothes which were unlike anything she had seen previously. One dress, a magyar style, had highly coloured wool embroidered bands round the neck, hem and sleeves; another in grey flannel, was embroidered in wools in royal blue, emerald green, bright orange and purple. These garments were an innovation at the time and had a strong influence on the senior students. She produced a great deal of experimental work herself and with her students, and was very fond of brilliant colour combinations of red, purple, pink, orange and jade for which she became well known.

The following remark was made by a critic in 1925 when reviewing a school exhibition at Croydon: 'We should like to temper our appreciation of this excellent show of students' work with the suggestion that their colour schemes are apt to run too much on the same lines and that in using several pure colours it is extremely important not to allow them an equal chance to sing their loudest'. Rebecca Crompton was keen also on monochromatic schemes and worked some of her most successful embroideries in whites, greys and blacks, using transparent fabrics. Her approach was vitally alive, as she possessed a dynamic personality, was very dogmatic at times but always stimulating. She worked students hard, those who were taught by her gaining a great deal, but she was very strict and anyone who slacked was ignored. Her experiments were worked sometimes on the domestic machine in straight stitching, combined with hand embroidery, as she was a pioneer in using mixed techniques and fabrics. She put silks, velvets, cottons and laces together, embellishing these with braids, buttons, cords and anything that could express her ideas. She utilised raw edges as part of a design and by the early thirties had revolutionised many of the previous thoughts on embroidery and dress in the schools of art. (Frontispiece and pages 148, 149.)

Summary 1920–1930

Prominent people

Paul Nash, painter, war artist, designer of embroidery.

William Tryon, painter, designer of embroidery

Sonia Delauney
Lanvin   } French embroiderers who influenced English work
Chanel

Ann Knox-Arthur

Louisa Preece

Marian Stoll

Mary Hogarth

Rosamund Willis

Madeleine Clifton

Isabel Catterson-Smith

Anne Brandon Jones

Mary Thomas

Rebecca Crompton

Societies, schools, exhibitions, events

1919 –33	The Bauhaus, Weimar closure at Dessau
1920	The Embroiderers' Guild – renaming of the Society of Certificated Embroideresses
1920 –22	School for teachers of needlework at the Victoria and Albert Museum, Joan Drew
1920	British Institute of Industrial Art formed
1921	Modern Embroidery Society, Edinburgh
1921	The Red Rose Guild
1922	Exhibition sponsored by the British Institute of Industrial Art – Victoria and Albert Museum
1922	Semi-private exhibition, Embroiderers' Guild
1923	Public exhibition, Embroiderers' Guild
1925	Paris Exhibition, L'Exposition Internationale des Arts Decoratifs et Industriels Modernes
1925	Independent Gallery Exhibition
1926	Arts and Crafts Exhibition Society, Burlington House
1927	Embroiderers' Guild Exhibition, Walker Galleries

1927 Modern Embroidery Society Exhibition

1927 The Clapham Trade School opened

1928 Arts and Crafts Exhibition Society Show

1928 Modern Embroidery Society, Edinburgh

1929 Votes for women over 21

Main types of embroidery

French influence in dress
Beading, embroidery, sequins
Aztec styles – geometric pattern
Appliqué of large flowers on dress
Machine embroidery, metal thread, in the trade
Peasant embroidery for clothes decoration
Patchwork of Sonia Delaunay – strong influence
Bolder work – wools on crash and linen
Bowls of circular flowers in felt, or surface stitchery, also fruit
Fine silk embroidery of flowers on clothes
Samplers of stitches and techniques still popular, as well as pictorial styles
Large hangings – portières
Darning on net, filet and hexagonal
Embroidery completely covering the material
Quilting popular
Copying of historic embroideries less in evidence
Canvas embroidery for upholstery
Influence of European schools of embroidery
Outlook much freer

Magazines and books

1920 *Samplers and Stitches*, Grace Christie

1920 *An Embroidery Book*, Ann Knox Arthur

1921 *Embroidery and Design in the New Stitchery*, Elizabeth Foster

1921 *Constructive and Decorative Stitchery*, Elizabeth Foster

1922 *The Embroideress* published by Pearsall and Co

1925 *Leaves from my Embroidery Notebooks*, Louisa Pesel

1926 *Simple Stitch Patterns for Embroidery*, Ann Brandon Jones

1928 *Needlework Through the Ages*, Mary Symonds and Louisa Preece

Many magazines started at an earlier date continued through the twenties and thirties

1920s *Stickereien und Spitzen*, well known to English embroiderers in the late twenties and early thirties

81 Far left: 1920. A sofa back embroidered on cream cotton, in floss silks in various muted colours. Chain stitch, cretan, buttonhole and stem stitches are among those used. The finely drawn flowers are typical of floral designs of the second and third decade of the twentieth century. The photograph shows a part of the border about 7 in. (18 cm) deep. *The Embroiderers' Guild*

82 Left: Early 1920s – Kathleen Harris. The panel is worked on natural linen in crewel wools. Many of the threads are hand-dyed and slightly mottled in colour. Dark red, salmon pink, bluish pink and dull pink predominate. Dark and light turquoise, cream, pale green, yellow ochre and fawn are also used. Among the stitches are herringbone, cretan, laid work, satin, long and short and buttonhole. 20 in. × 48 in. (50 cm × 121 cm). *Loaned by Elizabeth Vernon-Hunt*

83 Above: Early 1920s – Kathleen Harris. Detail from embroidered jacket. The fabric is a black satin-backed woollen, embroidered over the sleeves and 12 in. (30 cm) deep yoke, with fine trailing lines in whipped stem in cream and black mallard floss. The flowers are in a variety of colours – bright blue, pale turquoise, pink, magenta, red, gold, yellow and orange, with a little purple. The leaves are in yellow green, green and bright green. Buttonhole, broad chain, chain, cretan, stem, satin and close herringbone are among the stitches used. The side seams are decorated with interlaced lines in whipped stem. *Loaned by Elizabeth Vernon-Hunt*

101

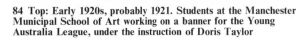

84 Top: Early 1920s, probably 1921. Students at the Manchester Municipal School of Art working on a banner for the Young Australia League, under the instruction of Doris Taylor

85 Above: The completed banner. *Loaned by Margaret Wimpenny*

86 Right: 1922–23. A curtain of blue linen with applied coloured linens; embroidered in brightly coloured wools. Designed and worked by Edith Bradley of the Manchester Municipal School of Art. *Loaned by Margaret Wimpenny*

87 Right: Early 1920s – Doris Taylor. A banner for the Girls'
Friendly Society designed by Doris Taylor. It was worked by the
Girls' Friendly Society, under the direction of Isobel Smail. The
background of the banner is in blue and white silk, embroidered
in bright silks and Japanese gold thread. *Loaned by Margaret
Wimpenny*

88 Below right: Early 1920s – Nancy Robinson. A dressing gown
embroidered in silk threads. *Loaned by Margaret Wimpenny*

89 Below: 1922– Doris Taylor. A banner for the Girls' Friendly
Society, in St Margaret's Church, Prestwick. The background is
gold with a cream lamé dress, green-blue pattern at the base and
slate blue stripes. Cream lamé strips edge the panel. Long cream
tassels are suspended from shorter blue green panels. The
lettering is mainly light on dark and the flesh is natural in colour.
The hair is dark brown with cream flowers. The cross is cream,
the crown in gold thread. *Loaned by Margaret Wimpenny*

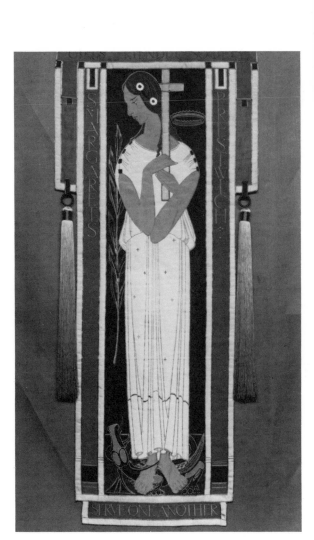

90 Left: Around 1920. A detail of embroidery on silk hexagonal net, worked in darning and filling stitches in silk thread. The negligée has patterns of flowers on the sleeves and back, with a gathered shawl collar, also embroidered

91 Above: Early 1920s. A detail of bead embroidery on a cream and black georgette dress, probably owned by a Mrs Liddle. The large rose, approximately $5\frac{1}{2}$ in. (14 cm) in width is in white, opaque glass bugle beads, smaller silver bugle beads and diamanté studs. The edges of the rose are worked in thin gold thread in buttonhole. The leaves are in white, opaque bugle beads and small, silver ones. The effect is of a silver rose. *The Costume Study Centre, Bath*

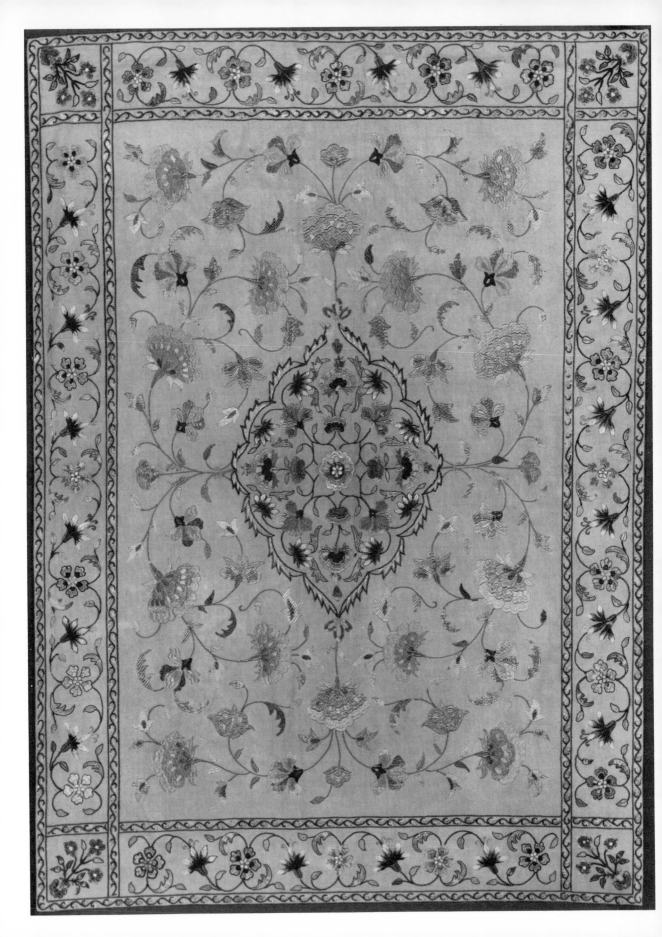

92 Left: Around 1920 – Louisa Pesel. A bedspread in natural linen, in many colours of silk embroidery. Bokhara couching, cretan, straight stitch, outline and other stitches are used. *The Embroiderers' Guild*

93 A detail of the above

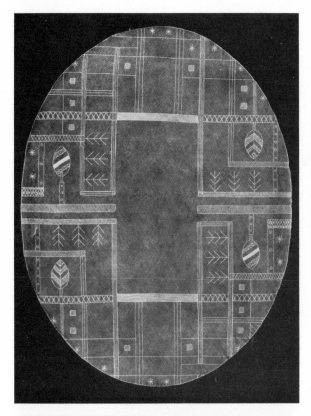

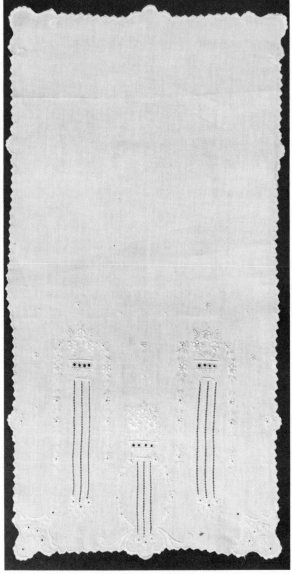

94 Top left: 1920s – Kate Louise Rosenstock, Leipzig. An example of darned net embroidery, typical of the style of work in Germany, and in Austria at the School of Lace and Embroidery, Vienna. The patterns are mainly geometric, simple and clear cut

95 Top right: Early 1920s. A chairback in white lawn, embroidered in fine cotton thread in padded satin stitch, eyelets, hem stitching, seeding and outline. The edges are scalloped in buttonhole

96 Left: Early 1920s – Isabella Kay. A fire screen of dark blue and grey hand-woven linen, embroidered in stout floss, in orange and blue with some green and cream. *Loaned by Margaret Wimpenny*

97 Right: 1920s – Doris Taylor. A panel of Noah's Ark in applied felts on linen, in a variety of colours. Couching, straight stitch, satin stitch and darning are used for the embroidery. *Loaned by Margaret Wimpenny*

98 Overleaf: Around 1922. A sequined and beaded dress, with a slightly dropped waistline, a V neckline and no sleeves. The garment of black net is completely covered in spangles and beads; the designs over the back and front, although different, depict a Persian garden. Part of the skirt is shown in the photograph. The Persian-type figures are in red, gold and blue square cut-glass beads which follow the contours of the body. Bright gold beaded outlines gleam against dark red-brown bead foliage on trees, one with a dark silvery trunk, the other with one in mauvish-blue beads. The bush between the figures is in reddish-brown beads. A large flower floating like a sun has dark gold petals with mauvish spines, and a centre of large, round gold beads. The base has horizontally sewn bands of red and gold beads, interspersed with spangles, each with a rough gold side and a darker side, sometimes the dark side showing, sometimes the gold. These spangles are sewn in vertical rows over the skirt, groups showing the gold side or the dark side. The top of the dress is in vertical rows of black sequins

99 1922 – Margaret Holden Jones. A brooch, one inch (2.5 cm) in diameter, worked in very fine petit point in silks, in a variety of colours on a grey ground, showing wild strawberries. The mount is silver. The brooch was exhibited in 1922 at an exhibition in the Victoria and Albert Museum sponsored by the British Institute of Industrial Art. It caused considerable interest

100 Around 1922. A detail of bead embroidery on a black georgette dress. The design consists of square cut-glass beads in pink, white and black. *The Costume Study Centre, Bath*

101 Left: 1923. An evening gown in bright yellow silk, overlaid with yellow chiffon and embroidered in gold beads and hand-stitched metal threads in a loose, uneven chain stitch. The geometric influence of Aztec pattern is seen in the use of zig-zags and triangles. *Victoria and Albert Museum, London*

102 Below: 1924. Dull-red silk georgette dress with bead encrustations in china beads, in dark green and blue-grey lines. The flowers are in pink, red, puce, lavender, turquoise and green. *The Costume Study Centre, Bath*

103 Right: A detail of the red silk georgette dress. *The Costume Study Centre, Bath*

104 Overleaf top: 1923 or 1924. A detail of pattern on the skirt of a pink georgette dress. The embroidery is worked on the Schiffli machine in black and white rayon threads in a repetitive design. The skirt is gathered over the hips on the dropped waistline, with a centre front panel from neck to hem left undecorated. The bodice has a yoke finishing in epaulettes and from yoke to hem on either side of the centre panel a row of small pearl buttons. The embroidery is 18 in. (45.5 cm) deep on the skirt, which is 21 in. (53 cm) in depth. The dress is sewn entirely by hand

105 Overleaf bottom: 1923 – Christine Smale. The yoke of a black crêpe-de-chine jacket embroidered in a variety of coloured silks in blues, reds, pinks, orange, purple and green, in chain stitch, cretan, buttonhole, stem stitch and others. The work was executed for the City and Guilds of London Institute Examination

106 Overleaf right: 1923 – Eleanor Joce. A sampler on dark natural linen – 'The Death of Cock Robin' – containing counted thread patterns and surface stitching. It is worked in darkish-red and black threads and the stitches used include long and short, running, back, chain, buttonhole of various kinds, herringbone, bullion, couching and seeding. Blackwork patterns frame the pictures. *Loaned by M Dyer*

THE DEATH OF COCK-ROBIN.

ALL THE BIRDS OF THE AIR FELL A-SIGHING & A-SOBBING
WHEN THEY HEARD OF THE DEATH OF POOR COCK-ROBIN.

ELEANOR JOCE. 1923.

107 Far left: 1925. A machine-embroidered curtain on black hexagonal cotton net, exhibited at the Paris Exhibition of 1925. The detail shows one corner; the other is less elaborate with the border continuing round three sides of the curtain, the wider border shown in the illustration finishing on the left hand corner. Appliqué of cotton fabric in yellow ochre is embroidered in red, yellow, pink, cream, blues, brown and fawn in chain stitch with some mossing, worked on the Cornely machine.

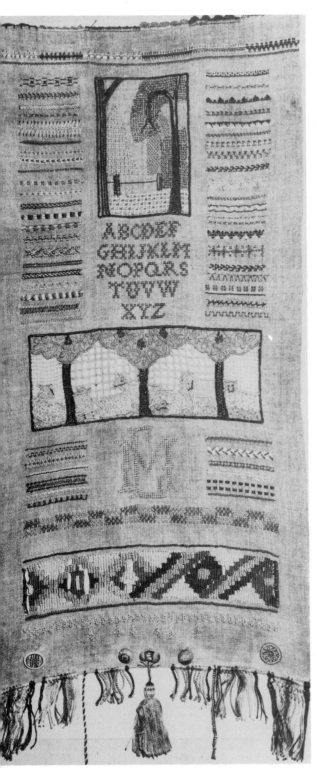

108 1925 – Mildred Lockyer. A sampler on dark natural linen, containing many stitches

109 Above: Late 1920s – Elizabeth Grace Thomson. A sampler on navy linen, embroidered in bright greens, yellow, red, blue, orange and mauve stranded threads. Among the stitches are German interlacing, buttonhole fern, chain and fly stitch. Ribbons are threaded through needlewoven bars and bars of fabric edged with buttonhole.

111 Above: Late 1920s – Louisa Pesel. A cushion in canvas embroidery, worked in long armed cross stitch, in a variety of colours

110 Above: 1926 – Mildred Lockyer. A curtain in dark green furnishing velour with decoration 48 in. × 42 in.
(122 cm × 107 cm) in size on the bottom. The sheep are applied in fawn velour with features in black. The large tree is applied in mid-brownish green velour, the horizontal stripe in a similar fabric. Buttonhole in wool in a lighter fawn secures the sheep to the background. The trees in outline are in several different bright greens in buttonhole and stem stitch, the applied tree is edged with bright greens, all in wools. The tree trunks are embroidered in black wool in buttonhole threaded with fawn, dark blue, green and light brown wools. The background between the tree trunks, in wools, is stitched diagonally in thick light green, couched with thinner yellow, while the horizontal lines are in running stitches in dirty mauves, dull blue-greens and mixtures of blue-green and mauve. The initials ML are on a sheep's back.

112 Right: Late 1920s – Kathleen Harris. Girl with a dog, 20 in. × 24 in. (51 cm × 61 cm). The panel is of tan hessian with applied felts. The girl has a red felt dress with orange and cream couched insets, flesh coloured felt skin and orange and cream hair, also couched. The dog is in a pale yellow-green felt. The ground is of navy and dark turquoise felt with cream couched whorls. The navy felt tree and bush have thin branches in chain stitch. The brown felt tree has turquoise and yellow-green felt leaves. Gold sequins add highlights. *Loaned by Elizabeth Vernon-Hunt*

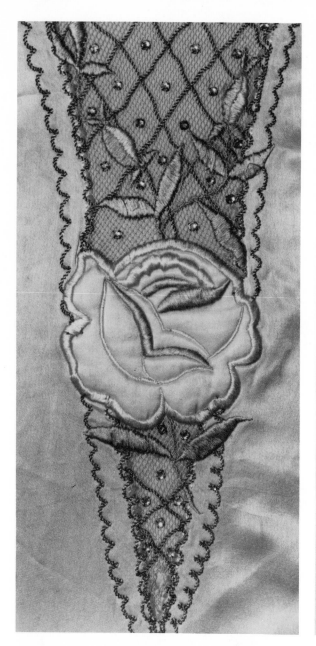

113 Above: 1928. A detail of embroidery on a cream satin and silk georgette dress. The panel, of which a small part is illustrated, is 22 in. (55.8 cm) long, from the neckline to the dropped waistline. The rose is 4 in. × 3 in. (10 cm × 7.6 cm) in size, padded and stitched on the Irish machine in satin stitch, in pink, pale pink and green; the leaves are green. The background of the rose is a coarse cream silk net over the cream satin, studded with diamanté. Fine cords of white silk and metal threads edge the panel and are stitched down by machine. Heavier cords make a lattice-like pattern over the net.

114 Above: 1927 – Duncan Grant. A banner designed by him, the fabrics cut out by Vanessa Bell, the work executed by Mary Antrobus, Mary Hogarth and Miss Elwes. A variety of fabrics are applied to a red background, in blues, yellows, green blues and off white. Stitches include couching, satin, chain, buttonhole, with pearls and other beads in several sizes. *Victoria and Albert Museum, London*

115 Below: Emmy Zweybruck. Drawing taken from a photograph of darned net, entirely in outline. *Stickereien und Spitzen*, **November, 1928**

116 Above: Late 1920s or early 1930s – Madeleine Clifton. Bedspread – red twill shapes on cream linen decorated mainly in a white linen thread using chain stitch. Feather, french knots, surface darning and pulled stitches are also used

117 1926 – Dorothy Angus. 'Sursum Corda', 19 in. × 17 in. (48 cm × 43 cm). The background fabric is double thread canvas, with surface stitches including cretan, double feather, chain, knot, stem, herringbone, satin, laid and couched thread work and other stitches. The threads used are soft embroidery cotton, pearl cotton and a little crewel wool. A design of six figures is prominently worked in turquoise and cobalt blue tones on a cream ground. The two side figures are in black sitchery. Three of the heads are golden yellow and three are black, all with grey features. Scattered throughout the design are lines of orchid pink, yellow ochre and orange stitches. *By courtesy of Ann Rider*

118 Late 1920s. A panel in applied felts and braids, in a number of bright colours, including blue, green, yellow, turquoise, red and others. The bowl or vase of flowers was a favourite subject for embroidery until the late 1930s. Many transfer patterns were issued on this theme in women's magazines and those on needlecrafts. *The Embroiderers' Guild*

The Thirties

In the 1930s the political as well as the economic situation was in a very uncertain state, with Nazism in Germany and Fascism in Italy growing. Unemployment in Great Britain was frightening and owing to the financial state of the country the National Government formed in 1931 cut the wages of many professional employees, such as teachers, and unemployment money. With the 1929 Wall Street crash the monetary situation became chaotic.

Design consciousness

In spite of this unrest the thirties showed a great advance in design and in aesthetic appreciation. A concerted effort was made to promote interest and to broaden the knowledge of machine- and hand-made goods, thus helping people to become design conscious and aware of their environment. Educational authorities, colleges of art and bodies such as the British Institute of Industrial Design sponsored exhibitions, lectures were given on textiles, furniture and other artefacts from Great Britain and from Europe. This helped to increase interest. Eventually standards of both manufactured goods and the hand-made articles benefited from these efforts, the thirties perhaps showing more design consciousness than any previous decade. Herbert Read wrote *The Meaning of Art* in 1931, in which he tried to give some idea of 'the elements' which went towards making a work of art; and the criteria on which aesthetic judgement was based. In 1934 he wrote *Art and Industry*, and during the thirties many books appeared on industrial art and design, architecture featuring in most of these along with interior design and textiles. Herbert Read disagreed with the separatist attitude towards fine art versus crafts and said 'The distinction between the fine and applied arts is a perilous one . . . beauty . . . inheres in any work of art irrespective of its utilitarian purpose or its size'. He also said that 'pattern alone does not constitute a work of art . . . but it does imply the distribution of line and colour in certain definite repetitions', and 'the real function of art is to express feeling and transmit understanding'.

People were becoming aware of this drive to bring art to them, thus helping them to understand and appreciate design. Embroidery was increasingly a means of decorating walls rather than of embellishing useful household objects or clothes. Many exhibitions were held, and by 1939 embroidery was a lively art, fostered by different educational institutions throughout the country and by various exhibitions. Design was becoming important in the applied arts, clutter was disappearing and a streamlined simplicity emerged, with obvious influences from other European countries.

Fabrics

Fabrics of quality were produced in this decade and a number of textile designers came to the fore, among them Alan Walton, Marion Dorn and Ben Nicholson, who was also a painter. Herbert Woodman, in a lecture in 1935 on textiles, said 'Many developments have taken place during this comparatively short time. If we are only considering contemporary fabrics, I think the productions of today are · far superior in every way to those made eight years ago'.

New fabrics on the market during the thirties were cloqué, a double woven cotton, and rayon which had improved in quality since the twenties and often took the place of real silk. Rayon satin was a favourite fabric, rayon marocain another. Nylon was produced in the USA at the end of the decade by Du Pont's, but was not used for garments until after the Second World War. With the now poor economic situation cotton took the place of the richer fabrics and embroidery on clothing disappeared, except for elaborate evening creations and accessories. Norman Hartnell, famous for his beaded and embroidered gowns, continued to make elaborately decorated dresses using sequins, pearls and other beads, with embroidery in silk and metal threads. His designs were mainly floral, and during this time he was appointed as dressmaker to HM Queen Elizabeth.

The glamour of the cinema and the film stars also influenced to some extent the dress trade and its decoration.

Techniques

A great deal of darning on coarsely woven fabrics such as that carried out in the late twenties and early thirties by Rosamund Willis exploited the fabrics and threads in a manner particular to embroidery, removing it from the idea that it was 'painting with the needle' – a phrase used to describe Roman embroidery of the third century AD. The use of techniques where the thread integrated with the fabric, changing its surface quality, such as darning, pulled work and other counted thread methods could be accomplished only with embroidery and did not imitate other crafts. These techniques were exploited during the first half of the decade, but embroidery became much freer later. (Pages 144, 145, 160.)

Household embroideries showed strong geometric patterns. There was also a great deal of line design at the end of the twenties and in the early thirties, usually of a pictorial nature. The leaping deer and the prancing horse were favourite subjects for embroidered panels, as well as the environment, featuring buildings and landscape. (Pages 159, 163.)

Different fabrics and methods were combined, machine embroidery grew in popularity, worked on the domestic sewing machine as well as on trade machines in the schools of art, in the trade schools and in industry (pages 148, 152, 162). The scene was one of increasing liveliness of outlook.

Branches of the Embroiderers' Guild

In 1931 the first branch of the Embroiderers' Guild was formed, the aim being to 'organise a local programme of embroidery events for members in their area'. This was the north-western branch which included Westmorland, Cumberland and part of Lancashire. Four other branches were formed by September 1939.

European influences

As European influences were now affecting British design and continental embroideries were shown in our exhibitions, it is important to mention some of the leading designers at this time in countries where the craft flourished. The French couture houses expanded, Chanel became famous for embroidered garments and simply cut suits. A very lively Italian designer, Schiaparelli, produced some most adventurous embroidered clothes with unusual colour combinations. 'Shocking' pink was her favourite, often combined with purple. She also designed some striking garments in black and white, one, a day suit with black leaves applied to white ripple satin, while a jacket in black wool had large mirrors applied. She chose subjects such as 'Comets' or 'The Circus' with the embroidery asymmetrically placed on the garment, sometimes wandering from the front to the back and worked with masses of beads in many colours, often with stitching and appliqué. (Page 153.)

Other embroidery on dress influenced by the peasant styles was seen in Great Britain at the end of the thirties. This was promoted indirectly by the craze in Austria and Germany for the healthy life which made these countries popular for vacations and led to the peasant costume cult, starting in England just before the Second World War.

The European influence in embroidery from Germany, Austria and Italy, also from Sweden, was noticeable in Britain during the second half of the thirties, with bold colour and simple, well balanced shapes, often in outline but strong in drawing and design. The developing influence was refreshing after the plethora of canvas embroidery, historical adaptations and derivative work prevalent during the earlier part of the century and even in the late twenties. Those who had seen the continental embroideries of the twenties were impressed by the fine net darning and the use of transparent fabrics for household articles.

Embroidery as a craft was practised in European countries before the First World War and was generally of a much higher standard than that being carried out in England in pre-war days. In fact Britain was producing in the late twenties styles that were seen in Germany in 1910, where whitework, with designs based on plant forms, was embroidered on satin in padded satin stitch and long and short stitches; cut and drawn work was also seen, these designs being applied to domestic articles, garments and accessories. Much of the ecclesiastical embroidery still showed an Art Nouveau flavour. Before 1914, wreaths of flowers, coiling stems and closely massed conventional flowers as well as linear patterns, some delicately worked, some heavier, were being produced. Herta Koch in Darmstadt in 1912 was embroidering closely knit floral patterns on dark blue or black grounds, using straight stitch and satin stitches in bright colours and in 1914 she produced some very free interpretations of flowers in vases worked in long vertical straight stitches only. This embroidery was far in advance of other work seen at the time.

There was a marked peasant quality in many of the foreign embroideries as most European countries had a heritage of folk art, with stitchery used to decorate costume and household articles. This tradition, but with a different interpretation, was carried on throughout Europe, gradually becoming more sophisticated as the twenties approached. In St Petersburg before the 1917 revolution Anna Somoff-Mikhailoff created some bags which were quite advanced in style, with detached leaves and flowers, made in double folded and ruched silk, with embroidery added, and also some with raised bunches of grapes made of padded silk shapes. These had a three-dimensional quality resembling stump work, but with a more contemporary feeling than that of the seventeenth century. After the war the schools of textiles carried on the pre-war traditions for a short time, working surface stitchery with a peasant flavour, illustrating folk and fairy tales as wall hangings. Sometimes the entire fabric was covered with stitchery in long and short, couching and satin stitches. Canvas work was popular and floral designs similar to those of pre-war days were still favourites. Decoration of costume and domestic articles, accessories and embroidered wall hangings continued. As the twenties advanced into the thirties the floral designs became simpler and less naturalistic, slowly changing to finely drawn, linear patterns based on a variety of plants. Simple leaf shapes, sharp and clearly delineated, almost geometric in concept, developed, sometimes combined with geometric pattern.

One of the most famous schools was the Wiener Werkstatte in Austria, where superb embroidery and lace were being created. Other schools, after the war, were set up in a number of places in Germany, Berlin, Frankfurt and Damstadt, in Budapest at the Textil Werkstatte and in Italy. (Pages 108, 121.)

Emmy Zweybrück, Else Köhler and other embroiderers well known in Vienna in the twenties were producing delicate darned net embroidery, linear design being particularly suitable for this technique. The embroidery was in fine white thread on white net, with solid areas and lines of darning arranged within leaf and plant forms and also in geometric areas around them. Filet net darning, quilting, organdie applied to organdie, pulled work with darned patterns were fashionable, and appliqué of net on fine fabric was seen in Austrian, German and Italian work, blouses of net being darned in exquisite patterns in the early twenties. Stripes were much in favour too at this time. (Pages 151, 168.)

Different continental schools produced their own styles of work and Emmy Zweybrück, a former pupil, later a professor in the Austrian School of

Embroidery and Lace, was a prolific worker and an excellent designer who had a considerable effect on her own and other countries, in the twenties and early thirties. Else Köhler was another designer from the Viennese school who used fine lines for her work. Fini Ehrendorfer was also from Vienna, while Kätie Louise from Leipzig, Suse Sandemann and Gerda Landsberg from Berlin were names well known to the British embroiderers who were selected to buy works for the Scottish art schools collection, known as the 1934 Needlework Development Scheme.

Each of these European artists had individual characteristics, such as Gertrud Schütz, trained in Berlin, who embroidered garments and panels using wools, with stitches covering the entire surface. She also worked on canvas. Much of the embroidery was executed finely in white on white with delicate effects; sometimes black and white were put together. Emmy Zweybrück produced a number of figurative embroideries during the mid-thirties – fine line drawings of peasant costume, using black outlines, with shaded flowers in long and short stitches, sometimes with black and white surface stitching, or with quilting to make very simple, modern statements. Italy produced examples of fine whitework and other kinds of embroidery of a similar nature and simple but striking designs were seen in Sweden and the other Nordic countries. These had a definite influence on English embroidery in the thirties and into the fifties. Ideas were becoming more abstract although the peasant and figurative styles persisted. The German magazine *Stickereien und Spitzen* published during the twenties and thirties in Darmstadt was instrumental in spreading many of the ideas developing in Europe after the First World War. Previously, this magazine had been published as *Stickerei-Zeitung* making a very lively contribution to embroidery.

In England **Rebecca Crompton** showed work in various exhibitions during the thirties. In 1932, her panel 'The Bathers' was mentioned by *The Needlewoman* magazine for 'The active spirit of our era, cleverly expressed . . . with all manner and different kinds of materials and embroidery stitches, finally completing the picture with diagonal rows of machining'.

In her experimental work she was most successful and her samplers were full of ideas. She used plain with patterned fabrics, lettering, flowers, leaves, buds, figures – in fact her subject matter was very varied and she appeared to be able to use anything in order to express her ideas. Her drawing was lively, her designs personal but she had a tendency to use looped lines to join isolated fragments together. These became a kind of cliché in the work of later embroiderers and a symbol of the thirties. They were seen long after Rebecca Crompton had introduced them into her own work and were used by others when ideas ran out, to fill gaps. (Frontispiece, and pages 148, 149.)

Her use of transparent fabrics led to another new idea which involved mounting separate frames with embroidery, placing them one behind another, thus obtaining real depth as well as the illusion created by her use of tones which were often enlivened with silver. With her mixed techniques and break away from rules Rebecca Crompton freed embroidery from the rigid outlook of the early part of the century. She produced a number of works entirely in white, white with silver thread and white organdie applied to white organdie, possibly influenced by the work of the continental embroiderers.

Rebecca Crompton was always seeking new approaches and was interested in everything that she saw. She was influenced considerably by some large hangings in appliqué being worked in the Glasgow School of Art. In 1935, she retired from full-time teaching to work for an exhibition in conjunction with a book on design that she was writing. Elizabeth Grace Thomson, a former student, introduced her to Dorothy Benson, who taught machine embroidery at Singer. Rebecca Crompton had been fascinated by the possibilities of machine stitching since she had seen some of the remarkable pictures produced at the end of the nineteenth century on the Singer domestic sewing machine. In her own work she had used straight stitching only, but she now went for instruction to Dorothy Benson, where she was taught to use the Irish and Cornely trade machines as well as the domestic sewing machine for embroidery. Rebecca Crompton designed many white embroideries, using transparent and other materials. A number of these were carried out by Dorothy Benson under her direction. Between 1936 and 1939 she came frequently to Singer for lessons, using the trade and the domestic machines for embroidery. She worked in a separate room where lessons were given and purchased the designs that Dorothy Benson carried out for her from the firm when the embroidery was finished.

In her exhibition Rebecca Crompton showed 126 works with a wide range of subjects, such as 'Cash in Hand' and 'Dog at Window'. Her book *Design for Embroidery* caused a great stir as its contents were far beyond the comprehension of many of the embroiderers in 1936. Ronald Grierson, a designer and weaver of rugs and an embroiderer said:

'This is a remarkable book which will probably be severely criticised by the majority of embroideresses. It represents the extreme swing away from traditional forms of design and technique in embroidery and for this very reason it is a valuable book. . . . It will give a lead and an immense amount of inspiration. . . . Mrs Crompton is a conscientious pioneer with an immense gift for design and an almost frightening facility for making a design from anything and with anything. Her main interest is with design and colour . . . stitching and technique are secondary . . . neither are her strongest points. She pays little attention to the purpose of the designs . . . a picture is but a small part of embroidery's scope and use. . . . By far the widest use of embroidery is to decorate the things we use everyday. . . . She proves once again that it is possible to make a picture without paint but she does not make an equally valuable contribution to embroidery as an applied art'.

Mary Rolleston, reviewing the same book said that it 'made an important contribution . . . and made a great appeal to those concerned with modern design for the twentieth century worker'. She also said 'Mrs Crompton is independent and refreshingly individual'. Her use of raw edges, as a part of a design, according to other reports, horrified the conventional worker.

In a pamphlet Rebecca Crompton wrote for Dryad's, she said 'Extreme neatness in design is not necessarily a good thing artistically. . . . In this plea for the application of more freedom in design I have avoided any reference to the way in which such suggestions might be applied to definite purposes'. She continued to conduct short courses in dress design and embroidery for the Board of Education but did not teach full time again.

Elizabeth Grace Thomson was a student of Rebecca Crompton but had been trained originally as a painter. When her father died, it was necessary for her to obtain a job which she did, but it involved the teaching of some embroidery about which she knew nothing, so she attended Croydon School of Art part-time. She exercised a very great influence on many people when she began to teach in the late twenties. She had enormous enthusiasm and high standards of achievement and many of her students at Bromley College of Art have become well known in different spheres connected with embroidery, including Beryl Dean, Iris Hills and Sylvia Green. (Page 152 and colour plate 9.)

She exhibited frequently in the thirties, and her embroidery 'The Blue Bird' decorated the cover of Mary Hogarth's book *Modern Embroidery* 1933, a Studio publication. She was an excellent draughtswoman and very keen to inculcate the idea of design arising from the qualities and use of materials. (Page 152.) With a sympathetic principal at the college, Arthur Baliss Allen, who was most co-operative, she raised the standing of embroidery and fashion to an important place in education. The college became well known for these subjects, particularly for machine embroidery. A technical assistant was employed, a Miss Evans from Singer, who worked under the supervision of Grace Thomson. When Miss Evans retired, Lilian Willey took her place. Iris Hills became an assistant in the department in 1937.

As one of His Majesty's Inspectors in the forties and a London County Council Inspector, Elizabeth Grace Thomson came in contact with many people and was able to help them to appreciate the qualities of fabrics, their possibilities for design, and the enormous scope of embroidery in all its aspects.

Rebecca Crompton's later machine work and also the development of machine embroidery was influenced by **Dorothy Benson** who became one of the most skilled technicians of machine embroidery that Singer employed. She started to work for the firm in 1916 and after doing odd jobs she began training as a machinist, partly using the domestic machine but mainly the Irish trade machine. The training was extremely exacting, the stitching often being examined with a magnifying glass for accuracy. She embroidered pictures and designs with some art content at first, but as the department became more commercialised trade work took over completely. This consisted of the embroidering of badges and banners, initial letters on linen and some ecclesiastical work.

Dorothy Benson, being now a superb technician, could interpret anything on the machine: fine canvas embroidery, lace and freely worked designs. She was promoted as head of the embroidery department and finally, in 1958, she was put in sole charge of the department where she stayed until her retirement.

In 1937 she was appointed as a specialist examiner for machine embroidery, for the Industrial Design examination of the Board of Education, this examination becoming in 1947 a part of the new National Diploma in Design which embraced the art examinations of the recently re-titled Ministry of Education. Machine embroidery was at this time a separate subject from hand embroidery and until the examinations were again re-arranged Dorothy Benson was the assessor for machine embroidery. She carried out a great deal of embroidery for the Needlework Development Scheme. Her book, the first one on the subject, entitled *Your Machine Embroidery*, published in 1952, explained the many ways in which embroidery on the domestic sewing machine could be accomplished.

Evelyn Woodcock taught in the Harrogate School of Art in 1928 where she produced with the students some excellent work in design and in embroidery. She was a brilliant designer of stained glass and later of embroidery and was an extremely competent draughtswoman. The embroidery in the school had a distinctive style with strong design and colour.

With the expansion of textile firms and the training of designers in various textile fields during the thirties, a number of artists became known for their embroidery, in fact this was a period of great development in the craft with lively exhibitions, raised standards and an increasing interest. Old prejudices disappeared, techniques became freer, machine and hand embroidery were intermingled and new names were appearing in exhibition lists.

During the early thirties Rosamund Willis executed a number of embroideries, usually based on her environmental studies. She was interested in buildings and landscape, working on linen with darning and canvas stitches. Lettering was incorporated into some of these. She carried out designs by other artists too and worked several embroideries for William Tryon, which he exhibited. (Pages 145, 161.)

Embroiderers in the thirties

Artists at this time produced embroidery of individuality and merit and contributed to exhibitions. Among these was **Kathleen Mann**, a great admirer of Rebecca Crompton with whom she had trained in Croydon School of Art. She took the place of Ann Knox-Arthur in the Glasgow School of Art for a short time. Her work was mainly pictorial with stylized figures and semi-geometric patterns, often carried out in appliqué in a variety of fabrics, sometimes applying organdie to an opaque ground (page 158). Her work showed the influence of Rebecca Crompton but with a more precise approach. Her floral designs had often a peasant like charm as she had researched into ethnic embroidery, writing and illustrating a book *Peasant Costume in Europe*, also one on appliqué and another on embroidery design and stitches. At this time there were few 'modern' books on aspects of embroidery. Hers were well received as they were clear both in text and illustration.

Ronald Grierson and his wife **Enid Grierson** had been weaving and experimenting with threads for some time. He became interested in embroidery on hearing about the exhibition to be held in the Victoria and Albert Museum in 1932. Between them they embroidered a fire screen for this exhibition, carried out in darning stitch in such an unconventional way that the Museum bought the work for their loan collection as an example of what could be done with a stitch. They produced as a joint venture a number of embroidered panels, some based on his woodcuts. These were shown by the Crafts Centre of Great Britain later on and by the Arts and Crafts Exhibition Society. (Page 154.)

Ronald Grierson also worked for industry as a designer of textiles and carpets and produced hand-woven rugs. The most important commission he and his wife carried out in embroidery was a very wide hanging, arranged in folds to go behind the altar, for the church of St Alban The Martyr, Oxford. This was worked in silk and fine wools. Enid Grierson carried out embroidery with her husband and together they produced many wall hangings until 1970. Their work was individual, characterised by both economy of line in the design and limited use of stitches in the execution. Satin stitch, stem, darning and tent stitch were used frequently. His colour was tonally good, often subtle in range, with designs which were basically simple, often worked on light backgrounds.

Talking of embroidery Ronald Grierson said that his interest in interior decoration led to his starting to embroider, as its chief function was to decorate. He did not agree with skilful copying for its own sake, and with limited time and the taste for simple architecture and furniture, he thought that stitching should be simple. He found canvas work monotonous, but surface stitching freer and flowing and thought that embroidery was a 'perfect medium for abstract designs', also that 'embroidered pictures and panels were ideally suited to the furnishing of our walls . . . and do not try to emulate oil or water-colour painters'.

Madeleine Clifton was well known in the late twenties and in the thirties. She had an individual outlook and was unswayed by fashion. She was an excellent technician and designer and preferred to plan ideas for a definite purpose as she felt that this was more of a challenge than embroidering panels without a particular place in mind. Her interest was in textures in stitches, with which she used appliqué. I remember her impressive bedspread in scarlet appliqué on white with scarlet and white stitches, shown in several exhibitions. She carried out ecclesiastical embroidery in which lettering was often incorporated, and as a memorial to her husband worked an altar frontal in the mediaeval manner for a church in Burghclere, Beaulieu, Hants. She did a great deal of patchwork and appliqué using a mixture of materials, often cutting up her own garments for this purpose. She also worked for the Women's Institutes in Kent, where she had quite an influence. (Page 121.)

In the early part of the decade Madeleine Clifton wrote an article for young students in *The Embroideress* advising them to learn to work stitches on the counted thread as this gave an idea of the relationship between the material worked on and the threads with which the work was done. She suggested that in designing and working more freely after this discipline, the result would have the quality of embroidery rather than of painting or print-making. She suggested also keeping the work developed equally throughout, building up step-by-step to avoid boredom when the hand lagged behind the mind. She advocated one stitch if using many colours on a piece of embroidery, or one colour, or tones of one colour if many stitches were employed.

Angela Bradshaw specialised in textile design, embroidery and theatre design, winning a number of prizes. As a freelancer she contributed many ideas and designs to newspapers and magazines. Among these were the *Manchester Guardian, Homes and Gardens, The Needlewoman* and *Stitchcraft*. She taught in Dundee College of Art from 1934 to 1950, training students for the Diploma in Art in Textiles and then until she retired trained students at Elizabeth Gaskell College of Home Economics (now the Manchester College of Higher Education) for the BEd in Art and Design, and also the BEd in Art related to housecraft. She was at all times interested in theatre design which she taught.

Lilian Dring worked in Fleet Street as a commercial artist before starting to embroider in 1931. Her first commission for embroidery was in 1934, and although she continued with commercial work, at the same time she produced a number of embroideries and exhibited with the Arts and Crafts Exhibition Society. (See pages 161, 164, 165.)

Ecclesiastical projects

In the early thirties an ecclesiastical project, the outcome of one of Louisa Pesel's activities, was carried out for Winchester Cathedral. She had designed and supervised the working in canvas stitches of cushions and kneelers for the private chapel in Wolvesey Palace, the residence of Bishop Woods. The result was so successful that it was suggested that similar embroidery should be undertaken for Winchester Cathedral.

Louisa Pesel and her friend Sybil Blunt worked together. Sybil Blunt designed the medallions for the cushions which showed a short history of Winchester from the seventeenth century to the 1930s. These medallions were framed in a variety of stitch patterns taken from Louisa Pesel's experiments, those she chose being used almost entirely by the Winchester Cathedral Broderers, formed in 1931. Wools were specially dyed to exactly the colours required, the backgrounds of the embroideries being in three different blues to give unity. By May 1932 many articles were finished and the project was completed by 1936.

The Cathedral Broderers dispersed with the outbreak of war, but Louisa Pesel carried on. She designed kneelers for the Lady Chapel, based on ancient tiles in the retro-choir. These were worked by girls evacuated from Atherly School, Southampton, to the Deanery.

Embroidery for the choir of Wells Cathedral was undertaken in 1933. A guild of needleworkers started to make covers for kneelers and hassocks and for cushions in the sub-stalls and seats in the presbytery. A decision was made also that the backs of the canopied stalls were to be covered with embroidery containing heraldic devices. Red and blue alternating backgrounds were chosen, with gold for the special seats of the Dean, Precentor, Archbishop of Wells, Chancellor and Treasurer.

A large body of workers was organised, some continuing in spite of the War. The embroideries for the canopied stalls were completed in 1948, the scheme almost finished by 1951.

The Dowager Lady Hylton was both the designer and secretary for the needlework in the choir. This was in five parts. The designs for the banners in the stalls with the special seats contained symbolic devices relating to each of the occupants, except the Dean. The remaining 31 were uniformly designed with a shield in the middle of each, commemorating some of the bishops who had officiated since 909, when the See was founded. For the Bishop's throne the main centre panel depicted St Andrew, the patron of the Cathedral.

The architect of Guildford Cathedral, Sir Edward Maufe, and his wife Prudence Maufe were inspired by the Winchester Cathedral embroideries and decided to embark on a similar scheme for Guildford. Louisa Pesel gave them advice on materials, but her ideas on design differed for this project, in that she advocated a basis of traditional English work. Lady Maufe wished to use contemporary history for 'the pleasure and interest of generations to come'. Most of the designs were by Sir Edward Maufe, his wife and some of their staff. Occupations, everyday objects, personal interests and other ideas were suggested, but all the designs had to be approved by the architect. The main idea for the kneelers was a dividing line diagonally across each one, symbolising the steep hill on which the Cathedral stood. The lower left triangle was in dark blue, the upper right one in white. The individual symbols were incorporated with the basic pattern. Workers chose their own stitches. As much of the work for the Cathedral was carried out after 1939, more information on the embroideries is given in Volume 2.

Exhibitions

Most art schools still included embroidery as a part of their curriculum and a criticism of the work in some of these was that design was good but that technique was poor, or vice versa. Freedom in execution, with an inventive approach, was not generally accepted at this time, careful technique still being of major concern among those embroiderers without art training.

In Scotland there was similar criticism although a high standard of achievement was maintained by the well known, established embroiderers who had been holding exhibitions during the twenties. At the Arts and Crafts Exhibition Society show in England, at Burlington House, in 1932, a review of the embroidery stated that there was a wider range of ideas than previously but that they were less advanced than those of central Europe. At this exhibition Rebecca Crompton showed lively work in appliqué with good ideas but which was criticised as being carelessly executed. Elizabeth Grace Thomson exhibited 'The Blue Bird', peasant like in design, inspired by the hand-woven fabric that she found, with a loose texture that suggested the technique. Colours were bright, worked in Mallard floss, a lightly twisted silk thread which contrasted with the woollen background. A variety of stitches and techniques were combined, including pulled work. The style was contemporary in outlook. May Morris showed a woven tapestry chair seat. One ecclesiastical embroidery only was shown, designed by Duncan Grant and executed by Mary Hogarth and Mary Symonds. The Fisherton-de-la-Mer Industries exhibited a coverlet.

Nora Unwin, a student of illustration at the Royal College of Art shortly before myself, remarked that 'appliqué embroidery is merely drawing and painting with needle and a piece-bag, instead of with brush and palette – let any sort of stitch and stuff imaginable be used if the result justifies it'. She was as far seeing as Rebecca Crompton in advocating the use of anything if it expressed the ideas of the embroiderer.

Abstraction

Abstraction in design was noticeable now, particularly in the simplification of ideas for canvas embroidery, where the use of flat areas of colour and pattern took the place of an attempt at three-dimensional reality rather in imitation of painting. One artist using petit point or cross stitch, Michael Senior, produced an exhibition of a number of abstract designs which were worked by Marjorie Craigie. Apparently the result was a lively and stimulating show but the critic remarked that it would have been better still if the designer and the worker had been the same person.

The schools of art, the Central School of Arts and Crafts and the Royal College of Art were beginning to influence standards in design and a number of students who were not necessarily embroiderers but later took up embroidery, were studying at one or the other of these establishments during the early thirties. Design for embroidery was mainly pictorial, but it became more stylized and abstracted as the decade advanced. A greater simplicity in outlook with the use of fewer stitches helped to present a clear cut effect. (Pages 149, 150, 152, 160.)

The Royal College of Art

At the Royal College of Art, and in other schools of art, embroidery flourished rather more as a means of decoration for interiors than for costume, with hangings and whitework 'pictures' prevalent. The work from 1931 to 1934 was generally fine, often on organdie, with shapes worked in outline, filled in with surface patterns, white on white, colour on white, darning in white on white net, or fine silk embroidery in colours on linen, where often the stitches almost covered the fabric. Buildings were popular as were pictorial embroideries of local scenes. The Thames or Kew Gardens were favourite subjects for London students while landscape and figurative subjects in surface stitchery or in appliqué were seen at exhibitions (page 159). Design showed a strong geometric tendency too, with reality reduced to its simplest forms.

Design, technique and fabrics

Embroidery for upholstery in the form of canvas work was seen throughout the decade, some of the most interesting ideas being semi-abstract or abstract in content, and based on a wide range of subjects such as musical instruments, mythology or rococo ornamentation sometimes reminiscent of the eighteenth-century cartouche, with muted colours such as pinks, greys and other delicate tones. Well-known textile artists designed for some of these embroideries. Wall hangings on a large scale, framed decorations and smaller framed pictures were all popular as they offered scope in the employment of different materials and techniques in a single piece of work. Buttons, braids, curtain rings, seeds, patterned with plain fabrics, silks, velvets and cottons, felt and hairy fabrics were used, several textures being put together; while appliqué, cut work, pulled fabric and surface stitchery were intermingled. The rigid, separatist rules whereby mixed techniques and materials must not be put together had gone in the schools, being disregarded by the adventurous student and artist. Appliqué was a favourite means of carrying out large pieces of work with surface stitchery in wools; smaller panels were often in organdie and other transparent fabrics, or darned net, or finely stitched on linen. Subjects included figures, landscape, buildings and stylized plants worked in silk or cotton threads. This greater freedom led to an interest being taken in embroidery as an art by the artist, as opposed to the embroiderer, trained in techniques rather than to appreciate the design necessary for work of an aesthetically high standard. (Pages 148, 149, 152, 156, 157, 158, 160, 164.)

Wall hangings: influence of design

'Art Deco' interior decoration with a more geometric approach to furniture design in tubular steel and glass was a suitable background for the many wall hangings now appearing. With the importation of continental textiles, glass, and laminated wood furniture from Finland, Great Britain was becoming aware of what was happening industrially in other countries. An exhibition at Dorland Hall in 1933, which I remember as outstandingly different, with clinically clean lines in the furniture, stressed the fact that design was an important issue. The Society of Industrial Artists which had been formed in 1930 held exhibitions and issued many books and pamphlets on design in the home and in industry and from the mid-thirties there was a great consciousness of design in Britain. The Dunbar Hay shop was a new venture, opened at this time to market the work of students trained at the Royal College of Art, among these being Grace Anderson (page 162).

Exhibition – Victoria and Albert Museum 1932

One of the most important milestones in the changing attitudes to embroidery was seen in an exhibition at the Victoria and Albert Museum in 1932, sponsored by the British Institute of Industrial Art. Unlike shows in which tradition was uppermost, a new, simpler approach to design was evident. Useful articles for the household and for dress were in the minority, with wall panels and hangings predominating. Pure stitchery, although seen in some examples, was less popular now than appliqué. In a review of this exhibition it was said that 'No society exists which would open the door to both hand and machine embroidery and close it to work based entirely on the traditional . . . there is a tendency to free the pace beyond the limitations of the craft'. It was hoped that the situation would readjust itself and 'that examples of enduring beauty will be more conspicuous . . . than they are today'. These remarks are interesting in that they refer to an exhibition where change and advancement were particularly noticeable. A certain starkness and simplicity in much of the design showed a continental influence but the sentimentality, the copying or imitation of historic embroideries was almost absent. Experiment, fresh ideas, a concern with wall hangings and panels instead of with household articles disappointed some of the critics as there were so few runners, luncheon mats and bedspreads on show. Besides this 'new' approach there were examples worked from transfers showing bunches of circular flowers worked in brightly coloured threads.

Several embroiderers already well known in the twenties exhibited; Madeleine Clifton showed her red and white bedspread (page 121) and Ronald Grierson a fire screen of a bowl of flowers, worked by his wife in whorls in tent stitch on canvas. It was said that some of the best exhibits were designed by Duncan Grant and Vanessa Bell, one of these being a panel inset into a mirror and worked by her in wools on canvas. The subject was of a three-quarter length figure of Orion sitting on a dolphin and playing his lyre. Another design worked in cross stitch in wools for a fire screen was a still life of a vase and a guitar, more painterly in style with a suggestion of light and shade. This was worked by Mrs Bartle Grant. Anthony Betts, a painter, exhibited designs in canvas work in wools, for a fire screen and a stool top, again the style somewhat painterly in effect; but a leather patchwork three fold screen, although pictorial, was strongly geometricised with angular forms. Rebecca Crompton exhibited her wall decoration, 'The

Creation of Flowers', saying that it was put together spontaneously without previous drawing and was 'an experiment in textures, tones and colours'. A variety of textured materials was used, some patterned, some transparent. The design 'depends on sharp contrast in colour and tone with subtleties in the various qualities of white . . . it is an example of inseparable design and technique'. She showed too a small panel in cut work. A screen using gingham in pink and white, with geometric flowers by Margaret Nicholls was innovative in idea (page 156). Grace Thomson, Rosamund Willis and Kathleen Mann, among others, exhibited, while William Tryon showed designs for rugs, worked by Mary Hogarth.

After the exhibition of embroidery at the Victoria and Albert Museum, which was crucial in the history of embroidery, Mary Hogarth produced her *Modern Embroidery*, a special spring issue for *The Studio* magazine in 1933, in which she said 'modern embroidery . . . should express this age. The technique should be governed by the design. . . . The forms in modern embroidery tend to be large and sweeping . . . the materials used are simple cotton materials, braids, buttons even'. She said that with the pace of life, speedier techniques such as appliqué were necessary, this being a good means of working when considering the large, bare spaces of the plain architecture in vogue, which required large decorations to soften their starkness. She saw the influence of the machine age in much of the work of the day but also that of tradition. She emphasised the fact that English work in the past was not copied from earlier times and that copying was not a means of creating liveliness. At the same time she thought that a student would do well to study the past and to copy one piece of historical embroidery completely, as an exercise and discipline.

She mentioned the continental work included in her book, which appeared to contain 'the modern spirit in its vitality, with the accomplishment of tradition'. She also referred to the new European design schools which had developed after the War, fostered by the Paris Exhibition of 1925.

From her remarks it would seem that Mary Hogarth thought that English embroidery was less advanced than that on the continent. In this she was perhaps right, as she was in wishing that embroiderers should be artists, not imitators.

Dress in the early thirties

Embroidery on dress was popular only until the middle of the decade. In the spring of 1932 decoration was confined to the shoulders and sleeves, which played a large part in garment design at the time 'in shape, length and treatment of cuffs . . . and many other features'. Up to 1935 embroidered blouses were in fashion and accessories such as bags and scarves were decorated, but when the more expensive fabrics were superseded by the cottons, such as cloqué and seersucker with their textured and patterned surfaces, these did not require further embellishment; also with the poor economic situation the luxury materials were beyond most people's purses while the cottons were within their limits. However, the embroidered blouse appeared again at the end of the decade in peasant guise.

Embroidery *magazine*

In December 1932 the magazine *Embroidery* was first published, its purpose 'to understand the beauties and historical characteristics of old work, in order to base upon them a really vigorous and well balanced new work'. The historical articles were excellent, the new work generally not very adventurous.

Change of style

The exhibition of the Embroiderers' Guild at the Walker Galleries in 1933 showed great changes between the old and the new styles and although there was still a traditional element, the 'moderns with their sense of design and colour, their freer approach, original ideas and outlooks' were regarded with keen interest. It was remarked that 'Even if this notice is one of disapproval, this is infinitely better than one of disregard'. It was also felt that materials had become more important than stitching in this show.

Instruction in embroidery flourished; at the Royal School of Needlework private lessons were given, as well as classes in technical skills. The

Townswomen's Guild held classes in embroidery and also exhibitions of work, as did the Women's Institutes which had advanced considerably although emphasis was on technique rather than on design and there appeared to be too much derivative or copied embroidery with little creative work. *The Needlewoman* magazine continued to issue designs reminiscent of the early work of the century as well as those for flowers, to be applied and sewn round with buttonhole stitches, but competitions were set by Clarke and J and P Coats. School competitions were also arranged, so real encouragement was given to those who wished to try out ideas of their own and to experiment with more contemporary styles.

Artists training during the thirties

Among students trained during the early thirties were **Dorothy Allsopp** and myself. I entered The Royal College of Art to pursue my studies of wood-engraving and book-illustration in the design school. There I met Dorothy Allsopp who had entered the college at the same time, also to study book illustration. Both of us attended the embroidery sessions tutored by Kathleen Harris, who had a wise philosophy in allowing students to experiment in whatever ways they wished. Dorothy Allsopp worked some small panels which I thought most advanced with their elongated, simplified figures and their technical excellence (page 160). Small embroideries were in fashion at this time and in contrast to these I carried out a large hanging of 'Adam and Eve'. She left the Royal College of Art after her training, having obtained a post in the School of Art in West Hartlepool; I left at the same time to take up a post in the School of Art in Cardiff. Both of us taught embroidery and wood-engraving among many other subjects. With us in the design school, **Grace Peat** (now Anderson) produced some very large hangings, geometric in style, in various depths of pile, with flat areas, in primary colours, worked on the Cornely machine. These hangings were particularly impressive in size, colour and technique, as machine embroidery was not a feature in the embroidery department at the time and her ideas appeared to be far beyond those of students studying embroidery at the college. Previously she was taught design by Frank Barber, whose designs for embroidery were carried out by Mary Symonds. Grace Peat also worked some figurative designs in outline on the machine, with a great freedom in drawing, and different from her previous styles of embroidery (page 162).

Aileen Molly Booker in the early thirties specialised in textile design, rather than in embroidery, as she considered that Miss Wright the tutor in embroidery at the Central School of Arts and Crafts, although an excellent technician, steeped in the William Morris tradition, was behind the times. According to Joan Lodge, who was training as an embroiderer at the time, Bernard Adeney, a textile designer and a lively artist, taught design to the textile students, including embroiderers, taking them from time to time round the Victoria and Albert Museum. Molly Booker attended his classes which she found stimulating.

Joan Lodge remembers that Molly Booker worked on hessian in vividly coloured crewel wools, covering the entire background with stitches, working stem stitch upwards on the material and chain stitch downwards: this she said was to avoid turning the material round. She was well known for her work, which was 'avant garde' in design, technique and colour. (Colour plate 8.)

She had an exhibition in December 1934 at Alex Reede and Lefevre Limited Gallery in London and showed 25 'sewed' pictures, among which were 'The Virgin and Unicorn', in beads on brocade, an appliqué fire screen, 'the Bride', 'Bathers', and 'My Aunt's Drawing Room'; also a canvas tray or table top. The screen in which beads, satin and pearls were used, 'White Bird with Beads', with silver materials and flames predominating, with the fabric sometimes completely covered with stitchery, was according to the review, an individual and exciting exhibit.

In 1935 Molly Booker wrote 'Embroidery Design' for a special number of *The Studio*. In this book she said 'too much attention is paid to stitchery, too little to design . . . at any embroidery exhibition it is distressing to see the amount of work done by people . . . who waste their time doing really beautiful stitchery on unworthy design'. She suggested a division of labour to improve design, which was: 'three days' design, one day life drawing, one day embroidery'. She also said 'the art lies in the right choice and application of stitches . . . in future the machine will play a much larger part in embroidery than it has done up to the present. The chief art in embroidery lies not in stitching at all, but in the design and right selection of suitable material and thread and in the gradation of tone and colour'.

Hebe Cox was also at this time at the Central School of Arts and Crafts and became one of the staff at the Royal School of Needlework for a short time before working in a studio. Hebe Cox exhibited with the Arts and Crafts Exhibition Society at Dorland Hall in 1935. She was also on the selection committee with Rebecca Crompton in 1938 for the Society's Exhibition. During the thirties she exhibited frequently, often canvas work panels, or stool tops, abstract or semi-abstract and very much in the more advanced style now developing. Her colour was often subtle, sometimes delicate, but never crude. She was a prominent and energetic worker, an excellent committee member who contributed a great deal to embroidery in helping to develop the craft within the Women's Institutes. With her lively approach and experimental attitude she unobtrusively helped women's organisations to raise their standards of work (page 165).

Beryl Dean had a wide and thorough training in a number of subjects, including embroidery, dress design, millinery and design in leather. Her first training at the Royal School of Needlework had given her meticulous technique in all her work, and she is a perfectionist (page 168). In the late thirties she assisted Elizabeth Grace Thomson, part time, at the Bromley College of Art where she had formerly been a student, until she gained a scholarship to the Royal College of Art. She continued to teach in the evenings, and became a professional milliner until war broke out, when she became a lecturer at Eastbourne School of Art.

Sylvia Green was an illustrator and was introduced to embroidery while at the Royal College of Art, through meeting Beryl Dean, who invited her to the Bromley and Beckenham School of Art. She taught part time there and also met Elizabeth Grace Thomson, to whom she says she owed a great deal. During the War years she did freelance work.

Valerie Bayford was a painter by training after which she studied embroidery with Rebecca Crompton. She was a very discerning artist, drew well and possessed an individual outlook, with great sensitivity. In spite of constant illness she was always cheerful and an excellent teacher. Her own work was precise and demonstrated a wide knowledge of stitches and methods, although she sometimes used a very limited technique on one piece of work. She was keen on pure stitching, often covering the fabric completely with laid work, long and short and filling stitches to give different tonal qualities according to the direction in which they were worked. She carried out embroidery for interiors, wall hangings and panels, often small, stitched in silks and framed. She tried various techniques including machine embroidery and was experimenting constantly, with subjects ranging from still life to figurative and imaginative compositions, usually using grey and subtle colours but showing good tonal contrasts. She liked to take one design and interpret it in several different ways. Valerie Bayford took Rebecca Crompton's place at Croydon School of Art for a short time in 1935 and also taught at the Royal School of Needlework, but her most influential teaching was at Reading University in the School of Art. She was a very sincere, thoughtful artist who would do her utmost for any student. She made a sound reputation for herself, with her own work and with her teaching.

Margaret Kaye started her training in printed textile design although she intended to be a mosaic artist. She studied stained glass, however, as there were no facilities for mosaics when later she entered the Royal College of Art.

She became inspired by Rebecca Crompton while still at Croydon school of Art producing a collage in the summer holiday before going to the Royal College of Art.

Averil Colby trained in an agricultural college and worked on a farm in the village where she lived. Illness forced a more idle life on her and she moved to another place, where her introduction to patchwork was fortuitous. From Muriel Rose, Averil Colby received the impetus to carry on with needlework. This interest she retained. Her work is well planned with an imaginative use of plain and patterned fabrics, good tonal contrasts and subtle uses of self-coloured patches sewn together to create patterns of lines. She works with traditional shapes, usually hexagons, from minute ones for pincushions to larger ones for bedspreads, using printed fabrics in such a way that she creates more patterns. Cottons are generally her chief fabrics.

Iris Hills trained as an illustrator and also studied embroidery at the Royal College of Art. After her training she obtained a part time post at the Bromley College of Art, assisting Grace Thomson, helping to build up a team of experts who worked in unison for a number of years.

Iris Hills was a co-ordinator of other people rather than an executant herself and with imagination and enthusiasm was able to get people to work with one another, but at the same time to develop the creative potential of the individual, whether staff or students. When she became a full time lecturer she organised the craft schools which continued throughout the War years and afterwards.

Frances Richards who studied mural decoration at the Royal College of Art also illustrated books while still a student and participated in exhibitions of paintings before she started to embroider. Many of her embroideries were worked during the 1950s.

A number of students trained during the late twenties and in the thirties started to embroider later. Some had careers broken by the Second World War while others had been trained previously in other subjects. The decade produced more artist embroiderers than at any previous time, a number of these becoming well known later.

Many articles were written on embroidery, on technique versus design, the latter being stressed, with an emphasis on originality as compared with copying and the use of transfers. Controversy over hand versus machine stitchery was also strong. Ida Dight of the Borough Polytechnic wrote several articles on machine embroidery in *Embroidery* magazine and in 1934 the Barratt Street Trade School took girls from 14 to 18 years of age, for a two-year course. This was technically excellent with instruction in hand and machine embroidery.

New ideas on the craft were emerging, encouraged by those who had trained in art institutions and who had begun to find embroidery an exciting study with its wider possibilities.

Exhibitions

In November 1934, the Modern Embroidery Society in Edinburgh held another successful exhibition in which Kathleen Mann and Louisa Chart showed work. The Red Rose Guild held a carefully selected exhibition during the autumn of this year too with an excellent standard of work. Other schools were also holding exhibitions, but it was said of the Royal School of Needlework with its perfect technique, that it lost the spirit of the ideas, resulting in a hard, poster-like quality in much of the work.

Design

Eleanor French, a well known embroiderer in the thirties who also edited *Embroidery* from 1938 until the Second World War, said that for many years embroidery had been the Cinderella of the applied arts, although the other crafts had new life and vigour.

'Embroidery for most people means laborious copying of some past design . . . or an even less intelligent method . . . that of the transfer, a design turned out from the factory by the thousand for the use of the thousand. . . . No speedy mechanical aids could be invented and as much leisure had gone, in the future simpler stitches with more subordination to the demands of the machine would be needed. Its future leads it nearer to legitimate art and further from craft. Unfortunately most artists have a feeling akin to contempt for embroidery . . . with very few exceptions it is not taken seriously by them . . . the reason being the feeble state of embroidery'.

With regard to design it appears that embroiderers in Great Britain were to some extent still living in the past, those without art school trainings finding it hard to appreciate the rather more advanced ideas of those who had an art background.

Needlework Development Scheme

A movement was inaugurated in Scotland in 1934, sponsored by J and P Coats and promoted by Colin Martin. This was the Needlework Development Scheme whose aim was 'to encourage greater interest in embroidery and to raise the standard of design'. It began as a scheme to assist the four Scottish art institutions which between them made a collection of 'modern' embroideries from different countries. A small book *Contemporary Embroideries*, undated but probably published in 1935, shows a delightful collection of foreign and British examples, with many different techniques and ideas. The book states that it was hoped that 'inspiration and fresh interest may be drawn from the technical excellence and imaginative qualities of the examples illustrated'. It also said that 'modern work will always owe something to the inspiration of the past, but to be vital and stimulating, it must belong to today . . . and the machine, no longer an enemy, is now a new tool in the artist craftsman's hand'.

The illustrations showed both foreign and British work, a number of examples by Emmy Zweybrück: white darned designs on fine net, coloured silk darning on white net, appliqué of silk with silk stitching, of figures with a charming, peasant like quality; also work from Munich and Münster and some from Italy. Among those from Great Britain were examples of work by Kathleen Mann of her simplified figures, shadow work on organdie, and a piece designed by Angela Bradshaw in a style very similar to the geometricised figure work of the mid-thirties, in organdie with net appliqué worked by Margaret Matthews. One piece by Molly Booker, a large hanging called 'Carnival', was illustrated, showing many people in a crowded composition that in the reproduction had strong tone values and a great liveliness. This was worked mainly in solid long and short stitches in wools. A piece by Rebecca Crompton, 'A Narrow Escape' was in a mixture of silk and wool appliqué, showing a simple figure running out of the picture, pursued by a goat with the background made up of triangles of fabric, a few stripes and back-stitched circles. Dorothy Angus's 'Penny Family' was taken from a drawing by a child of eight and was amusingly interpreted in wools on linen.

Exhibitions of these works were held at first in the four Scottish art schools, in 1935 showing acquisitions of 1934, and again in 1938 and 39. During the War the scheme closed.

Twentieth-century Needlework Exhibition

Mary Hogarth in her later years became the spokeswoman for a group of young artist designers and helped to organise several exhibitions. In January 1935 she attended the private view of the Exhibition of Twentieth-century Needlework at the Leicester Galleries. Joan Lavers was asked by Mary Hogarth to carry out some embroidery designed by William Tryon for the exhibition. A criticism of this show in *The Times* was that '. . . many of the works look as if they have been designed and then worked . . . the effect should surely be that of one operation, as if the design had grown out of the stitch. . . . Most of the workers seem to be more keen to realise the designs than to enjoy the needlework for its own sake'. It went on to say that '. . . the right direction for most of the designers represented . . . is to concentrate upon designing for machine production or upon assembling machine-produced fabrics. . . . Support is given to this belief by the fact that some of the most satisfying things in this exhibition are in terms of appliqué, or some kind of patchwork, rather than of stitching'.

A number of well known embroiderers exhibited work or carried out embroideries from designs by well known artists. William Tryon showed several pieces worked by different people. One was worked by Rosamund Willis, one by Mary Hogarth, and another by Mrs Middleton and Miss Standfast. The review went on to say that '. . . generally, the most happy relation between design and needlework, as understood, is in work of an earlier flavour . . . an altar frontal and a sofa cover by Mrs Madeleine Clifton'. Grace Peat who had recently left the Royal College of Art was mentioned for her cot quilt, while a panel 'The Golden Age' by

Molly Booker, a panel by Grace Thomson 'My Mother', and a panel by Ronald Grierson were all selected as worthy of notice. '. . . The general impression left by this lively exhibition', said the review '. . . is that by putting the emphasis on design in the abstract and reducing needlecraft to comparative unimportance, the new movement is asking for the machine.' Other artists showing work were Duncan Grant, with a panel worked by Mrs Bartle Grant, Claude Flight with a screen worked by Edith Lawrence, while Mary Hogarth showed a bag and Rosamund Willis a hanging 'Flight into Egypt'. Mildred Lockyer exhibited a cushion.

Exhibitions in 1935

More exhibitions were held and in March 1935 work by students from London schools and colleges of art were shown under the title of 'Art Schools and Industry' at the County Hall, Westminster, London. At this exhibition Hebe Cox from the Central School of Arts and Crafts presented a canvas stool top and Molly Booker several panels. The Borough Polytechnic, where Ida Dight taught, exhibited a machine embroidered bedspread, worked as a concerted effort by a group of students.

Other trade schools were developing both hand and machine embroidery at a high level of technical accomplishment and were also exhibiting work.

A Challenge Cup was presented to the Embroiderers' Guild in 1935 for yearly competitions among members. At this time too, the City and Guilds of London Institute asked to have a representative of the Guild on their examinations board. A diploma for judges was given in 1936, the first issued for judging embroidery.

Art and craft

The everlasting controversy over what constituted art and what craft, with reasons for the division between the two, continued as a lively subject for debate and Phyllis Platt writing on craft and art in *Embroidery*, trying to define the differences, said 'A craft is a technique used to produce things . . . for use. An art is a technique used to express an idea . . . not primarily concerned with use and . . . an artist's aim . . . the embodiment of an idea rather than the exercise of his technique'.

Ideas rather than technique were becoming important in the later thirties as more women with art training, but not necessarily in embroidery, were taking up the craft having realised its potential. Quite often they found their own methods of working. Several students from the Royal College of Art who took up teaching posts where embroidery was a part of the curriculum became interested although they had trained in different subjects, so had quite open minds on ways in which embroidery could be developed as an art form rather than just as a craft.

Embroidery was still omitted as a subject from the School Certificate examinations, although needlework was accepted in the syllabus. Complaints were being received about this omission and suggestions were made that it should be included as part of the art syllabus.

Transfers

Transfers were condemned as 'dull and lifeless' patterns, where the stitching was the important factor to the worker, and there was still a great deal of excellent technical expertise wasted on poor design during the late thirties even in the better exhibitions. However, the schools of art were now producing students who could go out to teach in part-time adult classes, in the schools and in other art institutions. These students as teachers helped to raise the standards in design appreciation and to make others aware of the great potential of embroidery as a creative medium, not just a therapeutic exercise.

The Surrealist Exhibition, 1936

The Surrealist Exhibition held in England in 1936, the first of its kind, had less impact here on crafts than it did in France, where Schiaparelli was considerably impressed by it, finding Dali's work inspiring. She produced some of her most fantastic ideas for accessories after this exhibition and collaborated with Dali on several of these.

139

Coronation robes and costume

The third coronation within the period 1851–1939 took place in June 1937, when George VI was crowned. His robes were similar to those of preceding kings. Ceremonial attire, the military uniforms and civil robes, the banners and ecclesiastical embroideries in Westminster Abbey, all richly decorated, gave to the spectacle a quality of richness obtainable only with embroidery (see pages 166, 167). The Queen's robe of purple velvet was similar to those of Queen Alexandra and Queen Mary, embroidered in gold thread with the national emblems, also with the Imperial Crown and two interlaced 'E's. The label of the makers was 'Ede and Ravenscroft, Founded 1689, Robe Makers, Court Tailors . . .'. The Royal School of Needlework executed the embroidery. The dress worn with the robe was in ivory satin, embroidered by Handley Seymour, in gold threads, diamanté and spangles. The design showed emblems of the British Empire and the Dominions, including the lotus, maple leaves, fern leaves and mimosa. Guests attending the Coronation wore dresses also lavishly embroidered. Princess Elizabeth and Princess Margaret wore smaller replicas of the Queen's robe (London Museum Catalogue – *Coronation Costume 1685–1953*).

Schoolchildren

During the latter half of the decade, work by schoolchildren was in evidence, sometimes dull and relying on transfers for design, but the exhibition at County Hall, London, in 1937 with an altogether different aspect, was lively and showed original works by children from a number of different areas. I saw this show and was very much impressed by both the art and the crafts and their vitality, embroidery being particularly exciting.

The exhibition Design in Education, devised by Frank Pick, sponsored by the Council for Art and Industry and put on at County Hall in London in 1937 was a great success, the aim being to show that if children in elementary schools were given the proper choice of materials, with their quality and attractiveness, these could help in an understanding of design. Elizabeth Grace Thomson was responsible for the selection of work done in Kent, in non-selective central schools and some junior art and technical schools. She also arranged many of the exhibits.

Through hearing about Elizabeth Grace Thomson's part in the exhibition Colin Martin of J and P Coats asked her advice on appointing an organiser for the Needlework Development Scheme. She suggested Dorothy Allsopp.

The standards of arts and crafts, especially embroidery, in the London schools had been raised since the 1930s through the inspiration of **Marion Richardson** who believed that through these subjects children could develop their talents considerably. As a London County Council inspector Marion Richardson was able to visit and to teach in all types of schools. She was a great educationalist and in 1917 was invited by Roger Fry to show in the Omega Workshops the work of the children she had been teaching. An exhibition which caused great interest was held in the Independent Gallery in 1923. Later as an art lecturer at the Institute of Education, London University, she trained art students. She became an LCC inspector for art and crafts and encouraged them in every way, embroidery being part of a special training from the infants to the senior schools. In 1937 she selected the children's work for the exhibition from the London County Council schools. She was very enthusiastic about writing patterns from which much good craft work developed. She also started a successful pioneer scheme to teach needlecrafts in prisons. She visited Benenden School part-time, too, where embroidery was a part of the syllabus.

Embroidery was introduced in 1938 as a subject for the School Certificate examinations, after a great deal of thought on its value in schools. At this time too, the Embroiderers' Guild was given a silver challenge cup for annual competition by senior schools, while junior schools were encouraged by the gift of a junior challenge cup, for which annual competitions were arranged.

Exhibitions 1937–1939

The Paris Exhibition of 1937 did not have the impact of the International one of 1925 when so many new ideas were seen. Instead of exciting contemporary embroideries being shown, ethnic embroidery was exhibited and although this was interesting, it was a retrogressive step in the eyes of the more advanced embroiderers.

The art schools continued to hold their annual exhibitions, some of the work being praised for originality and liveliness, some criticised for poor use of fabrics and workmanship. Well-known embroiderers continued to exhibit work; Rebecca Crompton, having taken up machine embroidery quite seriously after her training by Dorothy Benson, now showed work with more complicated machine stitching. Meanwhile Bromley School of Art was becoming known for its machine embroidery.

An exhibition of Needlework through the Ages in March 1938 at the Educational Museum in Haslemere must have been interesting according to the catalogue of exhibitors. Rebecca Crompton showed 'Peasants' Glory', a large free design, with a complexity of material held together by a vague pictorial idea; also her 'Creation of Flowers' and 'Flowers in the Rain', both experimental, with interesting 'placing of tones and textures'. Machine embroidery still caused controversy as seen by these remarks on 'Flowers in the Rain': 'which was a square of grey organdie worked in fine white machine stitching and silver . . . however, whatever may be the future of machine embroidery, many of us will wish that this exquisite design . . . should be worked out by hand'. Kathleen Harris exhibited a screen panel of 'the "feeling" of flowers in needlework, also a delicate little landscape in linen appliqué . . . with no suggestion of painting with the needle . . . a natural scene in carefully designed shapes and tones of linen, enriched with stitching . . . used with the restraint and discretion of real knowledge and long experience'. Joan Drew showed a wall decoration 'Spanish Dream 1935' in wools, with expressive colour and Molly Booker 'bizarre portraits of Creoles'.

At the end of the 1930s embroidery flourished and a number of exhibitions were held, the Society of Women Artists regretting that it did not receive more embroidery for its shows. The Arts and Crafts Exhibition Society was given an interesting review of its 50th exhibition at the end of 1938, in the spring issue of *Embroidery* 1939 in which there must have been really contemporary experimental work, together with the more conventional, careful stitchery with less vitality and a lack of understanding of design.

Of embroidery it was said that it was what is called '"modern", a term arousing enthusiasm in its exponents, indignation in its opponents, and . . . bewilderment in the average embroideress'. The indictments said that there was a disregard for use, traditional ideals of technique were flouted and natural and other forms were used with 'a disregard for beauty or verisimilitude'. Replies to these remarks said that use had never been the only reason for embroidery and that it was undertaken for the pleasure of planning and making, also many women now trained to draw and to design would experiment if embroidering. Lilian Dring's 'Common' was cited as an example (page 164). Elaborate stitching and repetitive work was 'not much seen in modern work'; a patterned fabric could be used as an alternative and beauty was really a personal matter, a question of 'the seeing eye'. Beauty varied in concept 'according to the spirit of the time'.

Needlework versus art

Phyllis Platt who wrote this review said that the two points of view '(1) from the aesthetic angle and the study of art, and (2) from the practice of needlework', were both needed for successful work. She went on '. . . The original designer with a sound art training who could produce advanced design and could experiment with materials was one type of craftsman, the other was the skilled needlewoman whose technique was perfect and who used conventional materials and stitches but was less experienced in design'. At this exhibition Beryl Dean showed her 'Madonna', (page 168), an example of experimental work using a variety of metal threads; Rebecca Crompton showed a small cutwork panel, in buttonhole, eyelets and chain stitch while Lilian Dring showed, as well as 'The Common', a nursery cushion; also exhibited was work by Kathleen Mann while Valerie Bayford was mentioned as showing an embroidery with the subject of three children. Some of the most successful experiments were by artists trained in other fields of art, who had turned to embroidery, such as Lilian Dring and Valerie Bayford, neither originally working in fabrics, while Margaret Kaye who also exhibited, was a lithographer and designer of stained glass. She showed 'Tiger', which was 'aesthetically pleasing, full of interesting textures and treatments, in deep, warm colour with rich detail'. Phyllis Platt summed up her review by saying 'we have today both the aritsts and craftsmen necessary to build up a vital new school of embroidery'.

The last number of *The Embroideress* was published in September 1939.

Dress in the late thirties

Embroidery on dress became fashionable again at the end of the thirties, particularly for afternoon and evening clothes and accessories. Appliqué in contrasting textures was seen such as velvet or leather on tweed, while evening wear was quite lavishly decorated. Some of the descriptions of garments by dress designers well known at this time sound magnificent, such as white tulle over silver lamé with the bodice embroidered in pearls and diamonds, or richly bejewelled, encrusted shoes, belts and boleros. A description of Eva Lutyen's collection says that 'it reaches Mogul splendours with sequin embroidered boleros copied from old Persian embroideries, gowns of white romain belted in fabulous, delicate embroidery and inspired by eighteenth-century tea cups, also a white moire coat embroidered in gold and glowing colours'.

The renewed interest in peasant embroidery developed too, fostered by the penchant for foreign travel, so peasant blouses, real or imitation were seen everywhere, often worked in primary colours of red and/or blue, in white on white, or multi-coloured. The embroidered apron became part of this craze, with the gathered skirt to complete the illusion.

In retrospect embroidery had advanced considerably as an art form from the early part of the century, with emphasis on ideas now of main consideration. Design and technique were merging successfully, the aesthetics of the subject were important and although the use of transfers and the copying of historic examples persisted among amateur embroiderers, those with some art training or an appreciation of the possibilities of the wide range of application of embroidery, were taking it up as an art and a craft. Through the difficulties encountered during the Second World War, with students and others directed into the forces, with supplies of fabrics and threads becoming limited, and with lessening of communication between colleges and schools (some of which were closed while others were evacuated), the arts could not flourish as they might have done had life proceeded normally. In spite of many obstacles however, embroidery did not die, but a new ingenuity was discovered that was a basis for further development during the fifties.

Summary 1930–1939

Prominent people

Herbert Read, author, critic, art historian
Alan Walton
Schiaparelli
Herta Koch
Emmy Zweybrück } European artists practising embroidery or designing for it
Else Köhler
Dorothy Benson

Elizabeth Grace Thomson

Beryl Dean

Iris Hills

Dorothy Allsopp

Constance Howard

Margaret Kaye

Frances Richards

Hebe Cox

Sylvia Green

Valerie Bayford

Kathleen Mann

Ronald Grierson and Enid Grierson

Angela Bradshaw

Lilian Dring

Aileen Molly Booker

Averil Colby

Marion Richardson

Schools, exhibitions, events

At the Royal College of Art and the Central School of Art standards were raised, influencing embroidery in the art schools and schools generally

1932 British Institute of Industrial Art – Exhibition, Victoria and Albert Museum

1934 Modern Embroidery Society, Edinburgh

1934 Needlework Development Scheme

1935 Arts and Crafts Exhibition – Dorland Hall

1935 Twentieth-century Needlework Exhibition – Leicester Galleries

1935 Work by London art schools and colleges and in industry

1936 First Surrealist Exhibition in England

1937 Coronation of George VI and Queen Elizabeth

1937 Exhibition of Schoolchildren's work – County Hall, London – Design in Education

1937 Paris Exhibition – lack of impact in comparison with that of 1925

1938 Exhibition at the Educational Museum, Haslemere

1938 Fiftieth exhibition of the Arts and Crafts Exhibition Society

1938 Embroidery was accepted as a subject in the General School Certificate examination

Main types of embroidery

Geometric design
Great variety of work and a considerable advance in ideas
Canvas embroidery for upholstery
Abstract styles beginning
Darning on coarse fabrics
Darning on net
Embroidery on organdie – white on white, interest in texture
Machine embroidery later in the decade
Line embroidery
Figurative work, highly stylized landscape and ideas based on the environment
Hangings and panels, appliqué, mixed techniques
Very little embroidery on garments
Consciousness of design more apparent in this decade than any hitherto

Magazines and books

1931 *Double Running or Back Stitch*, Louisa Pesel

1932 *Colour Pattern for Embroidery*, Ann Brandon Jones

1932 *Embroidery* magazine

1932 *Modern Needlecraft*, edited by Davide Minter

1933 *Modern Embroidery*, Mary Hogarth

1934 *Stitchcraft* magazine

1935 *Dictionary of Stitches*, Mary Thomas

1935 *Embroidery and Needlework*, Gladys Windsor Fry

1935 *Linen Embroideries*, Etta Campbell

1936 *Embroidery Book*, Mary Thomas

1936 *Design for Embroidery*, Rebecca Crompton

1937 *Appliqué Design and Method*, Kathleen Mann

1937 *Embroidery Design and Stiches*, Kathleen Mann

1938 *English Medieval Embroidery*, Grace Christie

1938 *Teach Yourself Embroidery*, Mary Thomas
Art in Europe I, Kathleen Mann
Art in Europe II, Kathleen Mann

1939 *The Embroideress* ceased publication

119 1930. A chair back in pale green blue linen, with applied white net, darned in tan, orange, yellow and cream stranded thread. The edges are in chain stitch or whipped. *The Embroiderers' Guild*

120 Around 1930 – Rosamund
Willis. The Goose Girl, a wall hanging
on Winchester cloth, worked in canvas
and darning stitches. Very brightly
coloured wools are used – pinks, blues,
dull reds, browns, mauve, dark green,
tan, grey, light orange, yellow green and
light green, black and yellow. The
design is based on a drawing by Frank
Barber. 84 in. × 54 in.
(213 cm × 137 cm). *Loaned by William
Angus*

121 Early 1930s. A fire screen of a crinoline lady within a circle. The dress is in purple chain-stitch, the bonnet in brown knotted buttonhole with a variety of coloured flowers, the tree trunk in brown stem stitch. Stranded cottons are used for the stitching. The result is typical of many transfer designs of the 1920s and early thirties. *The Embroiderers' Guild*

122 Right: 1931. A banner for the British Association for the Advancement of Science. This is the last banner made for the Association, for General Smuts. The background is a pinkish-brown damask brocade, with an applied blue brocade stripe. The flowers and leaves are in natural colours, all outlined in gold thread, couched down. The tree trunk is brown. The central landscape of rainbow and mountains is in natural colours with green sea. The lettering is black on cream satin, the tassels are dark blue. The emblems of the British Isles are incorporated in the design. *The British Association for the Advancement of Science*

123 Overleaf, top left: Early 1930s – Doris Taylor. A panel on natural linen, worked in wool and cotton threads in a variety of colours and stitches: blue, pink, scarlet, yellow, black and cream with buttonhole, chain, zig-zag, lazy daisy, herringbone, darning stitches and laid work. The design is very typical of the late 1920s and early 1930s, and is seen on household articles such as table runners, cushion covers and chair backs. *Loaned by Margaret Wimpenny*

124 Overleaf, bottom left: Early 1930s – Rebecca Crompton. A machine stitched panel in white on black organdie. Worked on the domestic machine. 16 in. × 10 in. (40 cm × 25.5 cm). *Loaned by Derby College of Art*

125 Overleaf, top right: Early 1930s – Rebecca Crompton. A panel with a background of coloured rectangles of fabric, in mauve and white stripes, red, orange, pale blue, green blue, greys, off white and yellow. Pink and white cords are attached by hand, as is the dark centre cord. The embroidery is in hand and machine stitching

126 Overleaf, bottom right: Early 1930s – Rebecca Crompton. A panel – 'Le Printemps'. Many different materials are used, including net, organdie, patterned and plain cottons, cord and ribbon. Machine stitching and hand stitching are combined; two layers of fabric, the upper one transparent, are framed together. Metal threads, cotton and silk threads are used, couched by hand. Herringbone, buttonhole, running and stem stitches are also used. Colours are delicate pale pinks, blues, black and whites being incorporated. 48 in. × 66 in. (122 cm × 168 cm). *Loaned by Derby College of Art*

127 Far left: Early 1930s – Mildred Lockyer. A panel entirely in black and cream fabrics. The background is a pale natural silk with appliqué in various fabrics including a grey with white stripes, a black transparent fabric with gold stripes, black ciré ribbon, cream satin ribbon, piqué and a greenish-grey American cloth-type, stiff fabric. The panel is embroidered on the domestic machine in black cotton in straight stitch, the ribbons and stiff fabric sewn down by hand. A frame of ribbon woven in black and silver surrounds the work. $13\frac{1}{4}$ in. × 17 in. (33.6 cm × 43 cm)

128 Above left: Early 1930s – Emmy Zweybrück. A runner, approximately 40 in. (100 cm) long and 8 in. (20 cm) wide, of white hexagonal cotton net, embroidered in darning stitches in white linen thread; transparent fabrics embroidered in semi-geometric patterns were typical of Austrian work during the 1920s and 1930s

129 Above right: Early 1930s – Emmy Zweybrück. A detail of the above runner. *Both the above loaned by Lois McBride, USA*

130 Above: Early 1930s – Elizabeth Grace Thomson. A machine-embroidered mat in metal threads, black thread and coloured thread. Worked on organdie on the Cornely machine. 7 in. (17.5 cm) in diameter

131 Right: 1930s – Elizabeth Grace Thomson. A panel, 42 in. (107 cm) square, in applied fabrics embroidered by hand, shown at the Arts and Crafts Exhibition Society. Stitches include buttonhole, satin, herringbone, couching and stem. Transparent fabrics overlap other fabrics. The design shows the abstract style which began during this decade

132 Above: 1930s – Schiaparelli. An elaborately decorated prune-coloured velvet jacket, embroidered in gold sequins, blue sequins, plate gold, metal thread and glass jewels. The oval jewels are in pink, pale blue and white, and the round ones in bright blue. The star-like buttons are in bright pink metal. *Victoria and Albert Museum, London*

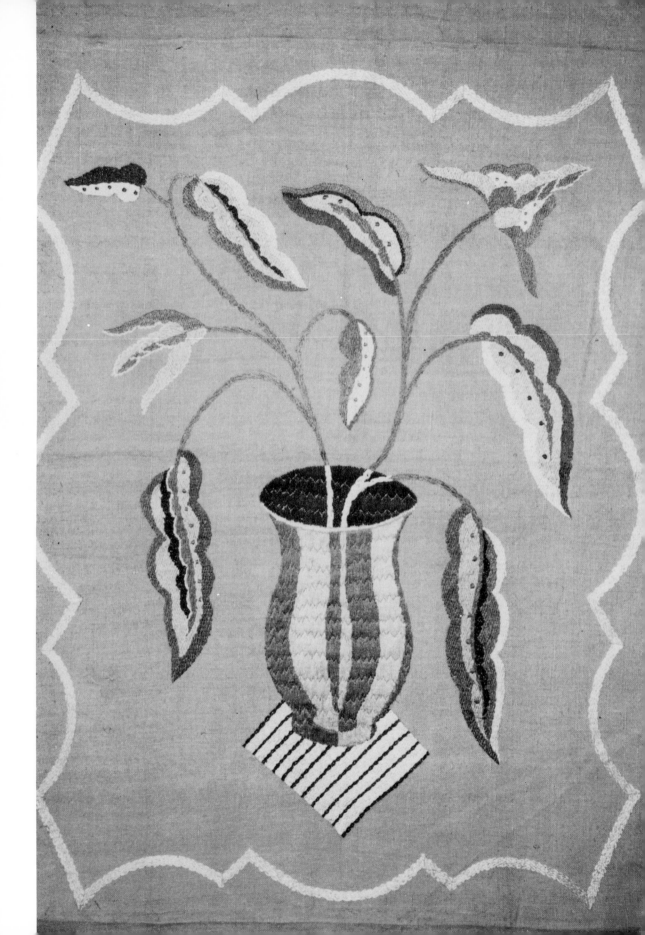

133 Left: 1932 – Ronald Grierson. A panel in yellow linen, worked in silks in creams, blue-greens, grey-greens and browns, in various stitches. *Victoria and Albert Museum, London*

134 Above: 1933 – Constance Howard. A circular panel 16 in. (40.6 cm) in diameter, on natural linen. The flesh is white 'tobralco' with painted shadows, the eyes are embroidered in blue, black and brown, and the lips are applied in pale tan shantung. The left-hand hat is in peach chiffon, with pearl beads and an orange feather, the hair is a dullish orange. The bow is a pinkish natural striped cotton, the dress silver American cloth. The right-hand hat is jade green cotton, with appliqué of natural shantung and silver American cloth. The hair is black, the dress with pearls in cream cotton. The lettering is in cream and very pale tan stem stitch. Other stitches are chain and couching

135 1933 – Margaret Nicholls. Embroidery based upon a Finnish rug. The background is in pink and white checked gingham. The squares are in light emerald silk, the spots in pink and red linens, the crosses in pink and blue wool. The dark triangular borders are in pinkish-mauve silk, the light parts white sheeting. Many other colours are used. The main stem is a green braid, the fine stems couched in wool

136 1933 – Marian Stoll. 'The Storm', 24 in. ×22 in. (61 cm ×56 cm). Four-ply zephyr wool on a thick linen background. Freely worked split stitch in black, greys and greens

137 Left: 1933 – Kathleen Mann. Embroidered panel, 51 in. × 72 in. (130 cm × 183 cm). Blue-green old Glamis fabric is used for the background, with appliqué in linens and square net, embroidered in wools and silks, mainly in couching, with some chain stitch and buttonhole

138 Above: 1933 – Freda Harlow. A landscape on linen, 14 in. × 16 in. (35.5 cm × 40 cm). The stitches more or less cover the ground. Various subtle greens, blue-green, yellow-green, grey-green and light green are used for the fields. The houses are in dusty pinks, ochres and grey blues. The trees are in various greens including olive and brownish-greens. Stitches include darning patterns, running, chevron, stem, a variety of buttonhole stitches, couching, whipping and backstitch

139 Left: 1934 – Dorothy Allsopp. A hand-embroidered panel on pure white linen, worked in silk threads in pale greys and other pale colours. The seagulls are in pure white buttonhole stitches with padded bodies, the dress is in Russian drawn ground. Other stitches are chain stitch, running and stem stitch. Approximate size $9\frac{1}{2}$ in. $\times 12\frac{3}{4}$ in. (24 cm $\times$ 32 cm)

140 Below: 1934 – Dorothy Allsopp. Cocktail tray worked on white pure silk moiré in filo floss in golds, pale yellows and spangles. Stitches include running, french knots, back stitch and straight stitch

141 Top right: 1935 – Rosamund Willis. 'The Annunciation'. The two panels, each 20 in. $\times 33$ in. (51 cm $\times$ 84 cm), are on unbleached linen. Arches are applied in cream organdie. The machine-made net robes are outlined in ric-rac and fancy braids. The passion flowers are in braid, whipped and feather stitched in pink stranded cotton; the flower pot is pink and yellow. The wings are in laid work in stranded cotton in turquoise with blue cross stitch, outlined in fancy braids. Couched gold thread outlines the features and the rays are in gold and silver. The halos, dove and stars are cut from aluminium sheeting. Pink and grey pearl beads and diamenté buttons add highlights. This panel was exhibited at the Red Rose Guild in 1935. *Loaned by the Gallery of English Costume, Platt Hall, Manchester*

142 Bottom right: 1934 – Lilian Dring. A coat rug, made from old coats, by cutting away the seams and rearranging the shapes already there into a design. Green and brown coats form the main shapes using the sleeves, fronts and sides of the garments. Other shapes were from tailors' pattern books and cuttings left over from dressmaking. Felt 'buttons' covered the buttonholes

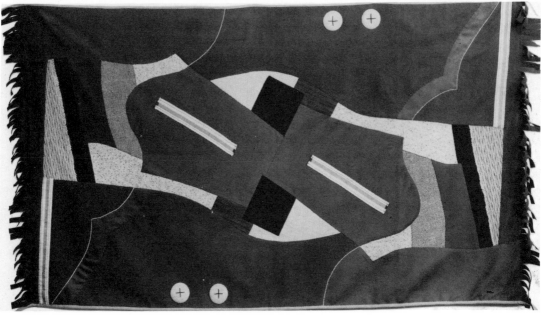

143 Left: 1935 – Grace Anderson (née Peat) ARCA. A panel worked entirely on the Irish and Cornely machines. The zigzag and satin stitch areas are worked on the Irish machine, the chain stitch and mossing on the Cornely machine. This design was worked by Grace Anderson as part of her Diploma project at the end of her third year at the Royal College of Art. 36 in. × 24 in. (91 cm × 61 cm). *Photograph – Studio Cellini, Colchester*

144 Above: 1936 – Kathleen Harris. A panel, 'Rolling Country', 12 in. (30.5 cm) square. The ground is cream linen, with hand-dyed applied fabrics for the fields, in pale tan and several greens. The panel is worked in filoselle silks, in dusty pinks, yellow-green and other greens, browns and dark blue-greens. The house has a dull red roof and grey walls. The lines across the fields are couched, other stitches used are herringbone, stem, straight stitch, some french knots, with a laid work roof. Couched grey clouds complete the picture. This panel was printed in *Embroidery Magazine* in 1936, in colour, to accompany an article on landscape, in which Kathleen Harris says that the effect is naturalistic but not realistic: 'Telegraph poles are used as a steadying influence on the curvature of the trees and the restlessness of the ploughed fields in the foreground, while the farmhouse brings a touch of human interest. It is springtime and the trees are only just bursting into leaf'. *Loaned by Elizabeth Vernon Hunt*

**145 Right: 1936 – Bridget Moss. The background of this panel is gold ribbon, with appliqué in organdie. The stitches which include couching, pekinese, knot stitch, twisted chain and threaded running, are in silk threads.
12 in. × 14 in. (30.5 cm × 35.5 cm)**

146 Above: 1937 – Lilian Dring. A 16 in. (40 cm) square coronation cushion for George VI. The ground is a striped rayon with applied decoration. The daffodils are in yellow felt with green shamrocks and mauve thistles on green velvet oak leaves. The cords are in red and gold. *Property of the Needlework Development Scheme*

147 Left: 1937 – Lilian Dring. An appliqué screen, 'The Common', consisting of five panels, each 72 in. × 18 in. (183 cm × 46 cm), based on drawings of the environment of Clapham Common. All types of green fabrics, dark to pale, are applied as are browns; the ponds are blue. The buses are in red American cloth with lace wheels and the winter trees in lace. The buildings are in tweeds and felts with some lace on the bandstand. Couching, buttonhole, fly stitch and couched cords are used for the embroidery

148 Above: 1936 – Hebe Cox. A canvas stitched panel, 'Pan', in navy blue, fawn, jade green, pink, yellow, rust and other colours. A wide variety of canvas stitches in silk threads gives a strong textural quality to the embroidery

149 Right: 1937 – Lilian Dring. A coronation cushion cover for Edward VIII, 16 in. (40 cm) square. The background is in ribbed rayon, with ER in purple velvet. The crown and orbs are in gold velvet. Running, back stitch and couching stitches are used for the embroidery. A dark red cord surrounds the cover

150 Above: 1937. The dress and robe worn by Queen Elizabeth at the coronation of George VI. The robe is similar to those worn by Queen Alexandra and Queen Mary, in purple velvet and gold threads, with emblems derived from nature; made by Ede and Ravenscroft, Robe Makers and Court Tailors. The dress is in white satin, embroidered in gold threads, diamanté and spangles. The emblems depicted are roses, leeks, thistles, shamrocks, maple leaves, lotus, ferns and mimosa. *The London Museum*

151 Above right: 1937. The dress worn by Princess Marina of Kent at the Coronation of George VI. The fabric is fawn lamé, woven with a feather pattern, emphasised by embroidery in spangles, beads and rhinestones. Made by Molyneux. *The London Museum*

152 Top right: 1937. A detail of the embroidery on the train of the coronation robe of Queen Elizabeth. Purple velvet is embroidered in different kinds of gold thread. The detail shows oak leaves and acorns in couched Japanese gold, pearls and plate, and shamrocks edged with twisted gold thread. *The London Museum*

153 Bottom right: 1938 – Alan Walton. A chair seat designed by him and embroidered on canvas in wools by Lady Glynn, in a variety of colours and stitches. *Victoria and Albert Museum*

154 1938 – Beryl Dean. A panel worked entirely in different kinds of metal threads, including gold, copper and other colours. The background is covered completely with the embroidery

Biographies

Abbreviations

ARCA = Associate of the Royal College of Art

NDD = National Diploma in Design

NDAD = National Diploma in Art and Design

FSIA = Fellow of the Society of Industrial Artists

C & G = City and Guilds of London Institute examinations

ATC = Art Teachers' Certificate

ATD = Art Teachers' Diploma

FSDC = Fellow of the Society of Designer Craftsmen

FIAL = Fellow of the International Institute of Arts and Letters

Dorothy Allsopp ARCA ATD 1911–

1929–31	Training at Chelsea School of Art
1931–35	The Royal College of Art – Design School and ATD
1935–49	West Hartlepool College of Art – full time lecturer in charge of women's crafts
1949–54	Expert in charge of the Needlework Development Scheme
1954–61	Senior lecturer in charge of fashion, embroidery and textiles – Hammersmith College of Art and Building (now part of Chelsea School of Art)
1961–76	Inspector of further and higher education (Fashion and Creative Studies) Inner London Education Authority
1976	Retired from the Inspectorate
1978	Chairman of the Examinations Subject Committee For Creative Studies for the City and Guilds of London Institute. Work purchased by the Victoria and Albert Museum

Dorothy Angus 1891–1979

	Training at Edinburgh College of Art – painting and embroidery. Assisted Louisa Chart in restoration work at the Palace of Holyroodhouse
1916	Appointed as a teacher, Carnegie Trust Craft School, Dunfermline
1920	Lecturer in embroidery, Grays School of Art, Aberdeen
1955	Retired from the school
Commissions	For the Needlework Development Scheme. A heraldic bedspread for Lord Glentar
1939–40	Panel – War Impressions owned by Dr Helen Russell. Also many others in private collections

M H Baillie Scott 1865–1945

Architect, designer of furniture and embroidery. Worked for continental clients. His houses were often 'Tudor' or 'country cottage' in style, with interiors in the comfortable cretanned upholstery of the nineteenth century. His wife worked some of his upholstery designs.

Valerie Bayford ?–1958

Training at Slade School of Fine Art – painting and drawing
Croydon School of Art – industrial design – embroidery
Board of Education

1933	C & G Embroidery I
1935	Part time lecturer – Croydon School of Art. Also part-time lecturer, Royal School of Needlework
Late 30s	Full-time lecturer, Reading University, Fine Art department. Chief examiner for the C & G of London Institute (embroidery) until her death

Vannessa Bell 1879–1961

Worked with Duncan Grant
Training as a painter at the Slade
A mural designer and interior decorator and designer for embroidery

1913–19	Worked at the Omega Workshops with Roger Fry. A member of the Bloomsbury Group

Dorothy Benson 1902–1977

1916	Entered Singer Sewing Machine Company. Carried out odd jobs. Later began training as a machine embroiderer and teacher of machine embroidery
1937	Appointed examiner as a machine embroidery specialist for the Board of Education Industrial Design examination
1939–45	In charge of the embroidery section in Singer
1947	Continued as an examiner for machine embroidery for the new Ministry of Education examination, the National Diploma in Design, in which machine embroidery was a separate subject
1958	Appointed to take charge of the complete department at Singer
1962	Retired from Singer
1963	The National Diploma in Design ceased
Publications	*Your Machine Embroidery*, Sylvan Press, 1952

George Frederick Bodley 1827–1907

Architect and designer of church vestments

1870	The firm of Watts & Co was founded by Bodley, Street and other architects, to make up their designs for ecclesiastical embroidery. Five frontals for the high altar in use since 1924 but designed from 1904 onwards

Angela Bradshaw

1924–29	Training at Manchester Municipal College of Art – textiles. Whitworth Scholar. Prizes for textile and theatre design – Royal Society of Arts

1929–34	Conducted own studio. Contributed articles and ideas to national newspapers and magazines, including the *Guardian, Glasgow Herald, Homes and Gardens* and Swedish papers
1934–50	In charge of women's crafts, Dundee College of Art
1950	Manchester College of Domestic Economy – lecturer
Commissions	Designer for the Daily Express Coronation Pageant, City of Dundee
	Pulpit fall – Glamis church, and others

Constance Brown (née Stone) ARCA 1881–1978

Training at Bristol College of Art
The Royal College of Art

1912	Head of Embroidery – Cambridge School of Art
1914	Embroidery accepted and hung in the Paris Salon – petit point roundel
1914	Award of Merit – Cambridge Arts and Crafts Society
1959	Retired to Bristol

Edward Burne-Jones 1833–98

Planned to enter the Church. Met William Morris at Oxford. Had a great interest in mediaevalism and decided to dedicate his life to art. He designed a number of embroideries, his style being influenced by Rossetti.
He produced ideas for compositions on a large scale and drew the figures for ideas for embroidery by William Morris.

Louisa Chart ?–1963

Training at The Royal School of Art Needlework

1906	Founder member of the Society of Certificated Embroideresses
1911–13	Appointed to teach embroidery at Wimbledon School of Art and Kingston-upon-Thames School of Art
1913	Lecturer in Embroidery, Edinburgh College of Art
1944	Retired from the College
Commissions	Repairing old embroideries – Palace of Holyroodhouse
	Set of chair seats – covers – for the Palace of Holyroodhouse
	A Bible Cover for Edward VII
	A Coat of Arms for George Watson Boys' School, and other works

Grace Christie 1872–1938

Training at Slade School of Fine Art – painting

1909	Appointed as the first tutor in charge of embroidery at the Royal College of Art
1921	Retired from the Royal College of Art in order to pursue her own work
1923–27	Was an examiner for embroidery for the City and Guilds of London Institute
Publications	*Embroidery and Tapestry Weaving*, John Hogg, 1906 republished by Pitman
	Edited *Needle and Thread* magazine published by James Pearsall and Co Ltd, quarterly from 1914. Four numbers were published before it was curtailed by the First World War
	Samplers and Stitches, Batsford, 1920
	English Mediaeval Embroidery, Clarendon Press, Oxford, 1938

Averil Colby 1900–

1918 Training at Horticultural College of Education

Worked temporarily restoring neglected gardens. Then on a farm and in the garden.
Illness led to quieter life. Went to Hampshire. Helped the Women's Institute with a patchwork bedspread, planned by Muriel Rose who became Craft Officer to the British Council.

1932 Interest in patchwork developed. Returned to the farm and there to date

Publications *Patchwork*, Batsford 1958, paperback edition 1976

Samplers, Batsford 1964

Patchwork Quilts, Batsford 1965

Quilting, Batsford 1972

Pincushions, Batsford 1975

Articles for magazines and journals

Hebe Cox 1909–

1931–34 Training at Central School of Arts and Crafts, C & G II
On the staff of the Royal School of Needlework.
Textile studio assistant.
Worked for and advised the National Federation of Women's Institutes with lectures and courses.
Founder member and trustee – Craft Centre of Great Britain
Member of the Arts and Crafts Exhibition Society

Publications *Simple Embroidery Designs*, Studio 1948

Embroidery Technique and Design, Dryad, 1954

Canvas Embroidery, Mills and Boon, 1960

Fifteen Craftsmen and their Craft, Sylvan Press, 1945 (contributor)

Contributed to *Oxford Junior Encyclopaedia*

English and Swedish Journals

Walter Crane 1845–1915

Illustrator, particularly of children's books, also a painter and an industrial designer. Great interest in plant growth. He was a powerful influence in the Arts and Crafts movement.

1884 A Founder Member of the Art Workers' Guild

1888 Designed many embroideries which were exhibited at the Arts and Crafts Exhibition Society, worked at the Royal School of Art Needlework and later by his wife
Lectured part time Manchester Municipal School of Art

1898–99 Principal of the Royal College of Art
Brought practising designers to the College to teach
An educationalist and concerned with the training of teachers and with art teaching in schools, where he promoted design

Rebecca Crompton 1895–1947

Training at Derby School of Art

pre–1922 In charge of embroidery and women's crafts, Northampton School of Art

1923 Head of women's crafts, dress and embroidery, Croydon School of Art

Late 1920s An examiner for the Board of Education Industrial Design examinations in embroidery and dress

1935	Retired from full-time teaching but continued with courses on dress and embroidery for the Board of Education
1936	Work in the Victoria and Albert Museum, some in Derby College of Art and some owned by private collectors
1937–39	Attended Singer for instruction in machine embroidery
Publications	*Modern design in Embroidery*, Batsford, 1936
Work exhibited 1977	'The Thirties' Victoria and Albert Museum
1979–80	'The Thirties' Hayward Galllery

Both retrospective exhibitions.

Embroideries were given to a Mrs Francis. When she died she included four of Rebecca Crompton's embroideries in her will. Two large pieces of work 'Spring' and 'Autumn Fantasy' given to a nephew in the Sudan. These are on loan to the Gawthorpe Hall collection. The others 'Head' 10 in. × 11 in. (25 cm × 28 cm) and 'Design' 12 in. (30.5 cm) square are in Shelton Lock, Derbyshire.

Lewis Foreman Day 1845–1910

Educated in France and Germany.
An industrial designer as well as designing for stained glass and embroidery, textiles and other crafts.
Lecturer at the Royal Society of Arts, also the Royal College of Art.
From 1890 art examiner and adviser to the Board of Education.

1870	Began his own craft business
1884	A founder member of the Art Workers Guild
1888	A founder member of the Arts and Crafts Exhibition Society. He wrote a number of influential books on design and pattern
Publications	*Pattern Design*, Batsford, first published 1903, reprinted 1979
	Nature and Ornament, Batsford, 1908
	Alphabets Old and New, Batsford, 1910
	Art in Needlework, Batsford, reprinted 1926

Beryl Dean MBE ARCA 1911–

Trained at The Royal School of Needlework

1930s	Bromley College of Art – embroidery, leather designs dress – Board of Education Examinations Royal College of Art Part-time teaching Professional milliner
1939–46	Lecturer, Eastbourne School of Art
1946–47	Lecturer, King's College, Newcastle. Own workroom for couture clothes
1952	Part-time lecturer, Hammersmith College of Art and Building – embroidery
1958	Ecclesiastical embroidery class commenced. Part-time lecturer at Stanhope Institute, London, courses and lectures throughout Great Britain and in the USA
1975	Awarded an MBE for services to embroidery
Commissions include 1940–45	Ballet Costumes and decor
	Work for the Needlework Development Scheme
	Banner – Chelmsford Cathedral

Red frontal – Chelmsford Cathedral

Three frontals – St Margarets Church, Kings Lynn

Set of vestments and frontal – St Martins Church, Dorking, Surrey

A cope for Guildford Cathedral

Frontal – St Giles Church, Northbrook, Illinois, USA

1974	Five panels – Royal Chapel, St George's Chapel, Windsor
1977	Festival cope designed by Beryl Dean and worked by students of Stanhope Institute

The Dean and Canon's copes; enthronement of the Archbishop of Canterbury

Two works for Sir Basil Spence, designed by Anthony Blee, worked by Beryl Dean

Work purchased by the Victoria & Albert Museum

Publications   *Ecclesiastical Embroidery*, Batsford 1958

Church Needlework, Batsford 1961

Ideas for Church Embroidery, Batsford 1968

Creative Appliqué, Studio Vista 1970

Embroidery for Religion and Ceremonial, Batsford 1981

Articles for magazines

Sonia Delauney 1885–

Ukranian by birth.
Trained as a painter.
Researched into colour cubism, which led to colour experiments in textiles, theatrical costume and some interesting patchwork garments.

Ida Marion Dight 1877–

Training at Camberwell School of Arts and Crafts for six years
Examinations – The Board of Education examination in advanced design; also drawing examinations connected with design
Obtained the bronze medal for embroidery in the National Competition
Teacher training – Attended lectures for teachers, on drawing. University of London lectures on the 'Art of teaching'
Worked in the trade

1905–7	Taught classes in design and embroidery for the London County Council
1907	Obtained the post of Art Mistress at the Borough Polytechnic
	Approved by the City and Guilds of London Institute as a teacher of embroidery
1919	From May to July worked with Messrs Reville and Rossiter in their dressmaking establishment
1924	In April visited Paris to study the methods of the Ecoles Professionelles
1928	First prize in a competition of industrial design, sponsored by Story and Co Ltd
1930	First class prize in a competition of industrial design sponsored by the Calico Printers Association, for a block printed design
Publications	Articles on machine embroidering in *The Embroideress* magazine, 1934

Joan Drew 1875–1961

Training uncertain, probably self taught. Carried out some book illustration in her youth. Gave a great deal of help to the Women's Institutes. Held classes in her own studio and also taught children.

1920–22	Taught the first classes in embroidery at the Victoria and Albert Museum

1926	Had portfolios of designs published by Pitman as an aid to the non-designer
1930s	Produced hand-embroidered rugs, banners and hangings
	Won the Embroiderer's Guild Challenge Cup
1978	Research by Joan Edwards culminated in an exhibition of her work at Loseley Hall, Godalming, Surrey

Lilian Dring ARCA 1908–

1922–26	Training at Kingston-upon-Thames School of Art
1926–29	Royal College of Art – Design School
1930	Commercial artist
1931	First embroidery leading to a commission in 1934
1935	Member of the Arts and Crafts Exhibition Society
1939–45	Worked for educational publishers, promoting ideas for evacuees
1947	Founder member of Crafts Centre of Great Britain
Commissions include 1951	Festival of Britain – panel designed by her, worked by Twickenham Women's organisations
1956	Many 'portraits of houses' the outcome of an embroidered house in 1956: ongoing projects
1957	First ecclesiastical commission
1959	Green Burse and Veil – Gloucester Cathedral
1961	Red altar frontal – St Mark's Church, Surbiton
1962	Chasuble – St Mark's Church, Surbiton
1965	Cope – church on Kew Green
1966	Cope – St Mark's, Surbiton
1967	White and gold vestments, Gloucester Cathedral
1971	Red 'presentation' stole – Vicar of St Mark's, Surbiton

Gladys Windsor Fry 1890–

Training at London art schools – painting
King's Prize winner
Embroidery C & G – Honours
Art Teachers Certificate, Board of Education
Art lecturer

Publications   *Embroidery and Needlework*, Pitman, 1935 5th edition, revised with new illustrations

Working Drawings for Embroidery, Pitman, 1955

Roger Fry 1866–1934

Trained as a painter and became an art critic

1901	Art critic for *The Athenaeum*
1905–10	Director, Metropolitan Museum, also the editor of *The Burlington Magazine*
1910–12	Arranged exhibitions of post-impressionist paintings
1913	The Omega Workshops were started, to produce well designed objects for daily use
	Became a brilliant critic
1919	The Workshops closed

Duncan Grant 1885–1978

Lived in India until the age of eight

Trained at Westminster School of Art and the Slade as a painter. Was also a mural decorator and designed many embroideries, for furnishing and ecclesiastical purposes.

1913–19 Worked in the Omega Workshops and was strongly influenced by Roger Fry's ideas

1920s and 30s Many canvas embroideries designed at this time, with a post-impressionist style, including mirror frames, screens and chair seats worked by Duncan Grant's mother.

A member of the Bloomsbury Group

Sylvia Green ARCA

Training at Frome School of Art

1935–38 Royal College of Art, Design School, embroidery and textiles

1938–46 Lecturer, South West Essex Technical College and School of Art, Costume, Fashion and Embroidery

Costumes made for the Ballet Guild

1947 Freelance book illustration

Part-time lecturer, Hammersmith College of Art and Building – embroidery only

Students from Mary Boon School attended these classes

1954 First commission

1969 Adult Education Classes, Inner London Education Authorities and Tutor at the ILEA annual Summer Workshops for craft teachers

1970s Part-time lecturer

1970s Part-time lecturer in ecclesiastical embroidery, creative embroidery, Stanhope Institute. Also in Putney

Mainly commissions, ecclesiastical with some secular embroidery

Publications *Canvas Embroidery for Beginners*, Studio Vista 1970

Patchwork for Beginners, Studio Vista 1970

Ronald Grierson FSIA 1901–

Training – worked as a designer for industry producing ideas for rugs and textiles

1979–80 'The Thirties' Exhibition, Hayward Gallery, South Bank, retrospective

Commissions (including works purchased)

1932 Fire screen exhibited and purchased by the Victoria and Albert Museum

1950 Large hanging for St Alban the Martyr Church, Charles Street, Oxford

Exhibited at the Arts and Crafts Exhibition, Victoria and Albert Museum

Commissions for woven articles for industry and private purchasers, both for ecclesiastical and secular purposes

Kathleen Harris (née Turner) ARCA 1880–1963

Training at Camberwell School of Art, with Ellen Wright, a pupil of May Morris, and Mary Houston

Specialised in embroidery and pottery

1913–21 Lecturer in charge of embroidery, Manchester Municipal School of Art

1921–39 Part-time lecturer, the Royal College of Art

Part-time lecturer, the Regent Street Polytechnic

During the War taught at the James Allen Girls' School

1933	Conducted the first course for the Embroiderers' Guild
1951–60	Editor of *Embroidery* magazine
	After retirement became President of the Sussex Branch of the Embroiderers' Guild
Publications	A guild book on *Altar Linen*

Freda Harlow ARCA 1909–

1928–31	Training at Northampton School of Art
1931–34	Royal College of Art – textile printing and embroidery
1934	Part-time teaching
1935	In charge of arts and crafts at Frensham Heights School
	Queen Ann Grammar School, York
	Lawnswood School, Leeds
1975	Retired
	Textiles sold to the Rutherston Collection

H. Harvey (embroidered from 1894)

Training as a painter in Rome and Florence
Executed a great number of ecclesiastical embroideries, mainly designed by other people: the Reverend Ernest Geldart, George Bodley, Mr Caroe, and others.
Cope – Bishop of London, designer G Bodley
Frontal – Chislehurst, designer E Geldart

Much later   Banner, Chislehurst
Frontal – St Barnabas, Walthamstow; designer Mr Caroe
Banner – Brompton Oratory
Cope – St Cuthbert's, Earls Court; also banner
Frontal – Marlow Church
Black damask vestments – St Matthias, Earls Court
And others

Iris Hills ARCA 1913–

1932–35	Training at Royal College of Art design school: illustration and some embroidery
1935–38	Part-time lecturer, Bromley College of Art. In charge of the 'Craft School'
1946	In charge of all the embroidery in the College. Worked with Lilian Willey and Joan Whayman
1955–61	Expert in charge of the Needlework Development Scheme
1961–66	Senior lecturer in charge of Fashion, Embroidery and Textiles at Hammersmith College of Art and Building
1967–77	Worked for the Inner London Education Authority
1957–72	Chief Examiner for the City and Guilds of London Institute examinations in embroidery, assisted by Elizabeth Geddes
Publications	*Introduction to Embroidery*, Victoria and Albert Museum, 1953

Mary Hogarth 1862–1935

Trained at the Slade as a painter. An excellent draughtswoman of architectural subjects

| 1921 | The Honorary Secretary of the Embroiderers' Guild |

1922	The Honorary Treasurer of the Embroiderers' Guild
	Taught for the Embroiderers' Guild
1923	Held classes at the Victoria and Albert Museum
1933	Resigned from the Embroiderers' Guild
	In later years the spokeswoman of a group of young artist designers
	Royal School of Needlework students lived in her house
Publications	*Modern Embroidery*, Studio Publications, 1933

Margaret T Holden-Jones ARCA, FRSA, FIAL, Hon FSDC, 1890–

1913–16	Training at Liverpool School of Art
1916–20	Royal College of Art – embroidery and calligraphy
1919	Royal College of Art – post graduate course
1922	Principles of teaching and school management
1923	Visited and taught in the USA
	Carried out various commissions
	Elected a Master Craftsman of the Society of Arts and Crafts
1922–23	Part-time lecturer at Blackheath School of Art, London
	Part-time lecturer at Goldsmiths College, University of London
1925–58	Lecturer in several schools and colleges
1940–54	Full time lecturer at North West Polytechnic, London; taught embroidery, pottery, calligraphy
1947	Founder member of the Craft Centre of Great Britain
1954	Retired from teaching
1960	Fellow of the International Institute of Arts and Letters
	Articles written on embroidery for magazines
Commissions	Include many for calligraphy, also:
	A colour wood-cut flower and insect book, now in the print room of the British Museum
	A water colour flower book in the manuscript department of the British library at the British Museum
	A petit point embroidered pendant ⎫ Both in the Victoria and Albert Museum
	A small petit point panel ⎭

Constance Howard MBE ARCA ATD FSDC 1910–

1925–31	Training at Northampton School of Art; embroidery, wood-engraving
1931–35	Royal College of Art; book illustration, Wood-engraving
1935–46	Full-time lecturer at Cardiff, Eastbourne and Kingston-upon-Thames Schools of Art
1947–75	Part-time lecturer, then full-time senior lecturer and principal lecturer in charge of Textiles/Embroidery, Goldsmiths School of Art, University of London. Many courses and lectures conducted throughout Great Britain, including those for the Ministry of Education, The Barry Summer School, and the Embroiderers' Guild
1955–63	Examiner for the National Diploma in design – hand embroidery
1958–69	Examiner for O and A Levels, Joint Matriculation Board: embroidery, dress design
1950s to date	Examiner for University Institutes of Education
1973–75	On panel for Council for National Academic Awards

1969–77	Lecture tours to Canada and USA
1975	Awarded the MBE, for services to Art Education
1978 to date	Assessor for Council for National Academic Awards
1978	Lecture tour to Australia and New Zealand
1979 to date	Canada and the USA

Work purchased by public and private collectors in Great Britain and abroad, including the Victoria and Albert Museum

Commissions

1951	Festival of Britain
1950s	Altar frontals – Makerere University, Kampala. Also stoles and burses.
	Banner – Mothers' Union, Lincoln Cathedral
	Designs for canvas work – Eton College Chapel
1960s	Throwover altar cover – Lincoln Cathedral
1973	Hanging – Northampton Museum
	Other commissions for secular embroidery
1974	Elected as a member of the Art Workers Guild

Publications

Design for Embroidery from Traditional English Sources, Batsford 1956

Inspiration for Embroidery, Batsford 1966

Embroidery and Colour, Batsford 1976

Textile Crafts (editor and section on embroidery), Pitman 1977

Constance Howard's Book of Stitches, Batsford 1979

Many articles in magazines and booklets, etc, including *Embroidery*

Selwyn Image 1849–1930

Training at the Slade School of Fine Art

| 1876–80 | Curate of St Anne's Church, Soho |

Stained glass designer and a designer of embroideries for the Royal School of Art Needlework

Founder member of the Century Guild and an influence in the Arts and Crafts movement

| 1910–16 | Slade Professor of Fine Arts at Oxford |

Edith John 1914–

Training at Doncaster School of Art

1935–47	Part-time teaching
1935–76	Part and full-time teacher, Doncaster School of Art (later college)
1972	Nantucket, USA, Summer school
	Short courses and lectures for the Embroiderers' Guild
1958	Commissions include a chasuble for the British craftsman exhibition, The Smithsonian Institute, USA

Work purchased by public and private collectors in Great Britain and abroad

Publications

Creative Stitches, Batsford 1967

Filling Stitches, Batsford 1967

Ideas for Needlecraft, Batsford 1968

Needleweaving, Batsford 1970

Experimental Embroidery, Batsford 1976

Margaret Kaye ARCA 1912–

1931–34	Training at Croydon School of Art, printed textiles. Board of Education, Industrial Design examination
1934–37	Royal College of Art – stained glass, fabric collage
1937	Full-time lecturer in printed textiles, Birmingham College of Art
From World War Two until 1977	Full-time lecturer, Guildford School of Art: lithography Freelance work Part-time lecturer, St Martins School of Art Part-time lecturer, Camberwell School of Art: lithography
1976	Visitor, West Sussex School of Art
1977	Retired from teaching
Collage Commissions	Include work purchased by Education Authorities, and by: The Victoria and Albert Museum The Festival of Britain The Contemporary Arts Society Murals for the Orient Line, for restaurants and private commissions Stained glass for private chapels, the Boltons, London; Chichester School; Formosa Rubey, Radnagé Restorations for the National Trust
Embroidery and collage commissions	Including ecclesiastical commissions for: Winchester Cathedral – Frontals Marlborough College, Ghana (for the Queen) Eastbourne, Manchester, Southampton and others Two ballets designed, one with John Cranko for Sadlers' Wells; one for the Ballet Rambert, the Mercury Theatre Work purchased by the Victoria and Albert Museum

Flora Klickmann (Mrs Henderson-Smith) 1880–1937

	Some art school training and possibly some musical education Became a journalist and worked for *The Windsor Magazine*
1908–30	Editor, *Women's Magazine* and *Girl's Own Paper*
1912–1920s	A prolific editor of magazines for children and adults, including the magazine *Stitchery*, issued quarterly as a supplement to the *Girl's Own Paper*. She also edited booklets: *Little Girls' Sewing Book* (1915) and *Little Girls' Fancy Work Book* (1919).

Anne Knox-Arthur

1912	Appointed assistant in the embroidery department, Glasgow School of Art, taking Ann Macbeth's place part-time Instructress for Killearn County Council, taking summer courses
1913	Summer courses
1914	Assisted Ann Macbeth, lecturing, and carrying out eight silk banners for the Henry Lauder Pipe Band
1915–16	Packages sent to regiment of Captain Bourdon (Professor of Architecture, Glasgow)
1920	In charge of embroidery, Glasgow School of Art
1930	Retired from Glasgow School of Art Exhibited at Lady Artists' Club

| 1933 | Conservation of Margaret Macdonald's panels for the Mackintosh Memorial Exhibition |
| Publications | *An Embroidery Book*, A and C Black, 1920 |

Ann Macbeth 1875–1948

1897	Training at Glasgow School of Art
1901	Became assistant to Jessie Newbery in the embroidery department
1904	Conducted Saturday classes for teachers
1906	Taught metalwork
1907–11	Taught bookbinding
1908	In charge of embroidery, Glasgow School of Art
1908–11	Lectured in many places
	Summer school teaching leatherwork and needlework at St Andrew's
1912	School of Art Diploma. Taught ceramic decoration and gave many lectures
1920	Went to live in the Lake District, but continued part-time teaching in Glasgow
1928	Retired from the School of Art
Commissions and work	Designed for Messrs Liberty, for Knox's Linen Thread Company and for Donald Brothers, Dundee
	Carried out a frontal for the communion table, Glasgow Cathedral, also a commission for a church in Hazelmere, and a purple frontal in St Patrick's Church, Patterdale
	Designed many panels and hangings, among these 'The Good Shepherd' and 'The Nativity', and also carried out private commissions
	She exhibited widely, at home and abroad.
Publications	*Educational Needlecraft*, (with Margaret Swanson) Longmans Green,
	The Playwork Book, Methuen, 1918
	School and Fireside Crafts, (with Mary Spence) Methuen, 1920
	Embroidered and laced leatherwork, Methuen, 1924
	Needleweaving, Simpson, Kendal, 1926
	The Countrywoman's Rug Book, Dryad, 1929

Frances Macdonald 1874–1921

1891–94	Training at Glasgow School of Art
	Married Herbert Macnair, architect
1909–11	Assistant instructress in the Saturday classes for embroidery in the School of Art

Margaret Macdonald 1865–1933

1891–94	Training at Glasgow School of Art
1900	Married Charles Rennie Mackintosh, architect. Had a very strong sense of design and carried out a number of embroideries. Her work was used in the interior of buildings designed by Mackintosh.
	Both sisters were excellent artists and embroiderers and together with their husbands, were known as 'the Glasgow Four'.

Charles Rennie Mackintosh 1868–1928

| 1884 | Apprenticed to architect's office – John Hutchinson |
| | Enrolled at the Glasgow School of Art |

1889	Junior Draughtsman – Honeyman and Kepple
	Minor designs undertaken
	Frank Newbery encouraged his artistic development
1896	The 'Glasgow Four' exhibited crafts, furniture and graphics at the Arts and Crafts Exhibition Society and many prizes were won
1897–1909	Glasgow School of Art was designed and built, but after this his work declined in ideas
1901–04	Redesigned the famous Willow Tea Rooms, Glasgow, owned by Miss Cranston

Kathleen Mann ARCA (Mrs Crawford)

1922	Training at Croydon School of Art: dress design
	Board of Education Industrial Design examination
1926–29	Royal College of Art
1929–30	Lecturer, Cheltenham School of Art
1930	Head of Embroidery, Glasgow School of Art
1933	Travelled to Italy for J & P Coats for the Needlework Development Scheme
1935–36	Central School of Art and Crafts
1948–	Part-time lecturer, Grays School of Art, Aberdeen
1955	External assessor for art for training colleges under Durham University
1958	Commission for set of mitres for the late Bishop Scanlan
1971	Elected member of Society of Scottish Women Painters
	Work purchased by public and private collectors, including Glasgow Art Gallery and the Links Collection
Publications	*Peasant Costume in Europe: Books 1 and 2*, A and C Black, 1931–36
	Design from Peasant Art, A and C Black, 1939
	Embroidery Design and Stitches, A and C Black, 1937
	Appliqué Design and Method, A and C Black, 1938
	Illustrations to *Scottish Costume* by Stuart Maxwell and Robin Hutchinson
	New Clothes for Old – wartime publication

May Morris 1862–1938

Younger daughter of William Morris

1885	Took charge of the embroidery workrooms of Morris, Marshall and Faulkner and Co
1893	Wrote *Decorative Needlework*
1905	Wrote a series of articles for *The Burlington Magazine* on the current exhibition of English embroidered vestments
1923	Left Hammersmith Terrace, where she lived, for Kelmscott Manor, to edit her father's papers

William Morris 1834–1896

1850	At Oxford where he met Edward Burne-Jones
1855	Decided to become an artist
1856–57	Worked for George Street, architect, and met Philip Webb
1856	Learnt to spin and weave
1861	Founded the firm of Morris, Marshall and Faulkner and Co in Red Lion Square
1865	Moved to Queen Square, Bloomsbury

1877	Gave his first public lecture – 'The Decorative Arts'
1888	First President of the Arts and Crafts Exhibition Society
1892	Founded the Kelmscott Press

Paul Nash 1889–1946

Training at Chelsea School of Art, and the Slade

| 1917–18 | War artist |

Painter and designer of textiles and embroideries during the twenties and thirties

Josephine Newall 1857–1922

1892	Founded the Fisherton-de-la-Mer Industries, Wiltshire
1904	Became a member of the Wiltshire Arts and Crafts Association
1907	Became a member of the Wiltshire Design and Industries Association

Jessie Newbery (née Rowat) 1864–1948

Training at Glasgow School of Art: drawing and painting

1894	Taught embroidery in the Glasgow School of Art
1895–99	Taught enamelling, and mosaic from 1896–98
1901	Ann Macbeth became her assistant while still a student
1906	Instituted an annual prize for embroidery
1908	Retired from teaching but continued to embroider. She exhibited widely, with work shown in Great Britain, on the continent and in the USA. It was apparently greatly appreciated in Germany.

Exhibitions

| 1893 | Exhibited metal work and an altar frontal at the fourth show of the Arts and Crafts Exhibition Society |
| 1902 | Showed an embroidered bedspread and a carpet in Turin |

Her work was very versatile and she embroidered dress accessories, household articles and ecclesiastical articles, including banners.

Mary Newill 1860–1947

1880	Awarded the John Surrow Wright Scholarship
1882	Taught in Birmingham School of Art
1919	Retired from teaching

Researched by Nancy Kimmins

A member of the Arts and Crafts Exhibition Society and The Bromsgrove Guild of Handicrafts

Commissions A frontal for Parkwood Church, Warwick and others

(*Researched by Nancy Kimmins*)

Louisa Pesel 1870–1947

Until 1900 studied with Lewis F Day

1903	Appointed as designer to the Royal Hellenic Schools of Needlework and Lace, Athens. Director until 1907
1908	Member of Society of Certificated Embroideresses
After 1913	Became an inspector of Art Needlework

1914–18	Helped to start a handicraft section in the Khaki Club
1920	President of the Embroiderers' Guild
1922	Started classes in Weymouth
1925	Started classes in Twyford, Hants
1926	Started the Yew Tree Industries, giving occupation to local people
1931	With Sybil Blount assisted in the designing and working of canvas embroideries for Winchester Cathedral
Publications	Stitch cards in colour for *Historic English Embroideries*, Lund Humphries, 1912
	Two portfolios of stitches published by Batsford; one from eastern embroideries, one from western embroideries, 1913. Examples of these are in the Victoria and Albert Museum
	Practical Canvas Embroidery, Batsford, 1929
	Leaves from My Notebook, in four series in 1930, as one volume in 1938
	English embroidery: series I and II
	Historical Designs for Embroidery, published posthumously, 1956

Katherine Powell 1890–1977

Born with only one hand

1906	Queen Elizabeth Grammar School Trained Hornsey School of Art, where embroidery was part of the general course
1908	City and Guilds of London Institute Examination, ordinary level
1910	School of Art Prize for holiday work
1911	Two bronze medals for embroidery, National Competition, Board of Education
1919	Silver medal – Advanced level City and Guilds of London Institute Examination Examiner Grace Christie Taught art and needlework in north London During the first world war she painted numerals and letters on compasses for the Royal Flying Corps.
1920	Taught in Barry, South Wales
1927	Taught art at Malvern Girls School, until her retirement in 1952
	(Research by Joan Edwards, *Embroidery*, winter 1978)

Marguerite Randall

Training at the Royal School of Art Needlework

1902	Received her Teaching Diploma Studied lace making in Bruges and Buckinghamshire Taught in the Normal School, Bloenfontein
1908	Taught part-time at the Royal School of Art Needlework
1912	Mistress of The Training School, Royal School of Art Needlework
1950	Retired

Frances Richards ARCA 1901–

Training at Burslem School of Art

1924–27	Royal College of Art, mural decoration, where she met Ceri Richards, the Welsh artist. Illustrated a number of books, obtaining some commissions when a student

Late 1920s	Taught at Chelsea School of Art
1930–	A considerable amount of embroidery, also painted in water-colours, from the 1930s to the present day. Work represented in museums and art galleries including: The Tate Gallery The Victoria and Albert Museum The National Museum of Wales Work bought by public and private clients
1975	Ten lithographs and a title page for Rimbaud's *Les Illuminations*, Curzon Press
Publications include	*The Acts of the Apostles*, Cambridge University Press, 1930
	The Book of Revelations, Faber and Faber, London; Scribners, New York; 1931

Marion Richardson 1892–1946

A pioneer in art and craft education in schools

1917	Invited to hold an exhibition at the Omega Workshops, of the work of children she taught
1923	An exhibition of children's work held at the Independent Gallery
1925	Art lecturer, Institute of Education, London University
1930	London County Council Inspector for art and craft
1938	Helped in the organisation of the exhibition of art and craft by children, held at the County Hall Pioneered a scheme to teach needlecraft in prisons
1940s	Evacuated with the London County Council Schools to Oxford

Rachel K Shuttleworth 1886–1967

Attended art classes in Paris. She was interested in social welfare and organised needlework classes. Her collection began with visual aids. A friend of Mr and Mrs Lewis F Day

1914–18	Secretary of Civic Arts Association
1921	Founded the North West Branch of the Embroiderers' Guild
1949	Awarded the MBE
1951	Founded the Fellowship of Church Workers, to repair and care for embroideries. Classified the lace collection of the Embroiderers' Guild. Wrote articles and collected items for the 'craft house' she was aiming to found
1952	Gawthorpe Hall, Lancashire, was offered to the National Trust and she became its caretaker. Her collection was moved to the Hall and students began to use the now famous study centre. Gawthorpe Hall became a recognised centre for the study of lace and embroidery, administered by Lancashire County Council

Eve Simmons 1884–

Training at Westminster School of Art: painting and at Tufton Street Archaeological Museum

| 1914–18 | Started to embroider, untrained
Produced embroidered dresses for children and waistcoats, bags and accessories for adults
Work in the Holborn Museum, Bath, on children's dresses: waistcoat and coat
Portière in the Whitworth Museum, Manchester
Embroidered sleeve in the Whitworth Museum, Manchester |

Marian Stoll

Working in the 1920s
Very little information on her background
Trained as a painter in the USA
Appears to have lived in England

1924–26 Exhibited in Oxford
Reviews of her exhibitions in the German Magazine *Stickereien un Spitzen*

Early 1920s Produced a great deal of work, illustrated in the German magazines. Wrote scathing articles on British embroidery, published by *The Embroideress* magazine

Margaret Swanson

1905 Attended the teachers' course at the Glasgow School of Art
Completed a 4th year post certificate course in colour and composition

1907 Obtained a certificate for Art Needlework

1910 An assistant in Glasgow School of Art. Lectured in various places and at summer schools

1911 Collaborated with Ann Macbeth on *Educational Needlework*

1911 Consulted by the English Board of Education, on needlecraft in girls' secondary schools in England

1913 Deputy to Ann Macbeth

1919 Needlecraft in schools

1926 Needlecraft and psychology
She was interested in education rather more than in practical work

Doris Taylor ARCA, 1890–1978

1905 Part-time Oldham School of Art

1906 Manchester Municipal School of Art

1907 Full-time student at Manchester Municipal School of Art.
Studied stained glass, painting, leatherwork, embroidery, wood carving.

1915 C & G: Advanced embroidery

1916–19 Royal College of Art

1919–21 Full-time lecturer, Hastings School of Art

1921–57 Head of Department in charge of dress and embroidery, Manchester Municipal School of Art

1950s Examiner for the Ministry of Education, Intermediate Examination in Art

1957 Retired from Manchester Regional College of Art (now Manchester Polytechnic)

Commissions Banners and other ecclesiastical embroideries:

Banner for The Young Australia League

Banner for the British Medical Association

Banner for the Mothers' Union

Banner for the Girls' Friendly Society

Private commissions

Ernest Thesiger CBE, 1879–1961

Training at Slade School of Fine Art: painting
Also The Guildhall School of Music
He became a well known actor

1914–18	Wounded and started a scheme to teach canvas embroidery to soldiers in hospital
1918–39	Experimented with various types of embroidery and preferred canvas work
1945	Vice patron, Embroiderers' Guild
	Interested in ecclesiastical work. Designed and worked two kneelers, Chelsea Old Church; wall hanging, Holy Trinity Church, Kensington Gore
	Restored eighteenth century chair seats, Temple Newsome, Leeds. Made a large rug at the age of 81.
Publications	*Adventures in Embroidery*, Studio, 1941 revised 1947

Mary Thomas (née Hedger) 1889–1948

Training as a musician
No training in embroidery

1912–14	Fashion artist, *Pictorial Review*, New York
1916	Returned to Great Britain. Joined the Women's Royal Nursing Corps
	Later, joined staff of *The Gentlewoman* magazine and became fashion editor
1927–36	Editor, *The Needlewoman* magazine
1936	Left *The Needlewoman* to concentrate on books
Publications	*Dictionary of Embroidery Stitches*, Hodder and Stoughton, 1934
	Embroidery Book, Hodder and Stoughton, 1936
	Teach Yourself Embroidery, Hodder and Stoughton, 1938
	Knitting Book, Hodder and Stoughton, 1938
	Book of Knitting Patterns, Hodder and Stoughton, 1943

Elizabeth Grace Thomson 1895–1981

Training at Royal Academy Schools: painting

1920s	Croydon School of Art: embroidery and dress design
	Assisted Rebecca Crompton part-time in her classes and on courses
Early 1930s	Became a full-time lecturer, Bromley School of Art.
	Developed embroidery and dress design from a small to a large department.
	Became Head of Fashion and Crafts, Bromley and Sidcup Schools of Art
1937	Responsible for Kent children's work – exhibition *Design in Education* promoted by the Council for Art and Industry
1939–46	Organised classes for Bromley School of Art
1946–52	Appointed His Majesty's Inspector of Women's Crafts – the first to be appointed
	Conducted a number of courses for the Ministry of Education, on fashion and embroidery
1952–61	Inspector of Women's Crafts in further and higher education for the London County Council
1961	Retired
1932	Victoria and Albert Museum exhibition

Phoebe Traquair 1852–1936

Lived in Ireland
Training at Dublin School of Art, painting

1873	Married and career interrupted
	Drew fish skeletons and other objects for the National History Department of the Museum of Science and Art, Edinburgh, where her husband was keeper
1879	One of her few surviving embroideries, a table-cover

1895–1902	Most important work – a four-fold screen in the National Gallery of Scotland. The screen was Exhibited at the Arts and Crafts Exhibition, 1903
1904	St Louis International Exhibition
Commissions	Decoration of the mortuary – Sick Children's Hospital, Edinburgh Social Union
1893	Mural decorations – Catholic and Apostolic Church, Edinburgh. Completed in 1897.

Mural painter, embroiderer, enameller, illuminator and jeweller. She received commissions for illustration and illumination. Collaborated with Sir Robert Lorimer, in the early twentieth century, carrying out enamelling and painting. Examples of her work are in the Victoria and Albert Museum

Rosamund Willis (Mrs Angus) ARCA 1903–1979

1921	Training – Cambridge School of Art. Embroidery with Constance Brown ARCA
1924–27	The Royal College of Art. Then with Heals for a short time
1929–36	Lecturer, Armstrong College, Newcastle
1936–38	Principal, Luton College of Art
World War Two	Guide lecturer with the Arts Council, for which she organised exhibitions

Commissions	
1957–60	Four panels and a reredos, St Ninian's Church, Aberdeen
	A banner for St Mary's Church, Great Shelford
1970s	Set of High Mass Vestments, designed by George Pace, St Olave's Church, York
	A panel depicting Brechin Castle for the Countess of Dalhousie
	Various exhibitions from the late twenties and local shows after 1960 in Aberdeen, Edinburgh, Harrogate and York

Evelyn Woodcock ARCA 1898–1978

	Training at Scarborough School of Art
1925–1928	Royal College of Art, Diploma in Stained Glass
1928 or 1929	Lecturer – Harrogate School of Art. Spent her whole teaching career there
1960	Retired from Harrogate School of Art
Commissions	Pictorial Street Map – Harrogate Corporation
	And other works

Bibliography

BATTERSBY, Martin, *The Decorative Twenties*, Studio Vista, 1969

BATTERSBY, Martin, *The Decorative Thirties*, Studio Vista, 1969

BOOKER, Aileen Molly, *Embroidery Design*, Studio, 1935

BRANDON-JONES, Ann, *Colour Patterns for Embroidery*

CHRISTIE, A H, *Embroidery and Tapestry Weaving*, John Hogg, 1906

CHRISTIE, Archibald, *Pattern Designs*, Clarendon Press Oxford, 1910, Dover, 1969

COLBY, Averil, *Quilting*, Batsford, 1972

CROMPTON, Rebecca, *Modern Design in Embroidery*, Batsford, 1936

DAY, Lewis F, *Art in Needlework*, Batsford, 1926

DREW, Joan, *Portfolio of Embroidery Pattern Designs*, Pitman, 1926

JONES, Mary Eirwen, *A History of Western Embroidery*, Studio Vista, 1969

EDWARDS, Joan, *Bead Embroidery*, Batsford, 1966

FRY, Roger, *Vision and Design*, Pelican, 1937

GLAZIER-FOSTER, Elizabeth, *Constructive and Decorative Stitching*, Pitman, 1927

GLAZIER-FOSTER, Elizabeth, *The New Needlework*, Pitman, 1921

HALLS, Zillah, *Coronation Costume, 1085–1953*, Her Majesty's Stationery Office, 1973

HOGARTH, Mary, *Modern Embroidery*, Studio Publications, 1933

HOWELL, Georgina, *In Vogue*, Condé Nast, 1975

HUGHES, Therle, *English Domestic Needlework*, Lutterworth Press, 1966

JOURDAIN, M, *English Secular Embroidery*, Kegan Paul, Trubenere and Co Ltd, 1910

KLICKMANN, Flora, *Home Art Series, Girl's Own Paper* and *Woman* magazine, 1912

KNOX-ARTHUR, Ann, *An Embroidery Book*, A and C Black, 1920

LAVER, James, *The Liberty Story*, Liberty & Co, 1959, reprinted 1971

LEVY, Santina, *Discovering Embroidery of the Nineteenth Century*, Shire Publications, 1971

LILLEY, A E & MIDGLEY, W, *A Book of Plant Form and Design*, Chapman Hall, 1895

MACBETH, Ann & SWANSON, Margaret, *Educational Needlework*, Longmans Green and Co, 1911

MACCARTHY, Fiona, *All Things Bright and Beautiful, 1830 to today*, Allen & Unwin, 1972

MANN, Kathleen, *Appliqué Design and Method*, A and C Black, 1937

MANN, Kathleen, *Embroidery Design and Stitches*, A and C Black, 1937

MASTERS, Ellen, *Book of Art Needlework*, Henry and Co, late 19th century

MORRIS, Barbara, *Victorian Embroidery*, Barrie and Jenkins, 1962

MORRIS, May, *Decorative Needlework*, 1893

NAYLOR, Gillian, *The Arts and Crafts Movement*, Studio Vista, 1971

OMAYA, Mario, *Art Nouveau*, Studio Vista and Dutton, 1966

PAULSON TOWNSEND, W, *Embroidery or the Craft of the Needle*, Truslove & Hanson, 1899 and 1907

PEVSNER, Nikolaus, *Pioneers of Modern Design*, Pelican, 1960

PROCTOR, Molly, *Victorian Canvas Embroidery*, Batsford, 1972

READ, Herbert, *The Meaning of Art*, 1949

RISLEY, Christine, *Machine Embroidery*, Studio Vista, 1973

SWAIN, Margaret, *Historical Needlework*, Barrie and Jenkins, 1970

THOMAS, Mary, *Dictionary of Embroidery Stitches*, Hodder and Stoughton, 1934

THOMAS, Mary, *Embroidery Book*, Hodder and Stoughton, 1936

TSCHUDI-MADSEN, S, *Art Nouveau*, World University Library, 1967

WARING, Mary E, *An Embroidery Pattern Book*, Pitman, 1931

WHITE, Palmer, *Poiret*, Studio Vista, 1973

WINDSOR-FRY, Gladys, *Embroidery and Needlework*, Pitman, 1935

Magazines, Catalogues, Periodicals and Booklets

Ancient and Modern Embroidery, Catalogue of Glasgow School of Art, 1916

The Arts and Crafts Exhibition Society Catalogues, 1893–1899

British Institute of Industrial Art, Catalogue of Exhibition, 1932

Catalogue of Embroiderers given by the Needlework Development Scheme, 1965

Catalogue of The Glasgow School of Art Embroidery, 1894–1920, Glasgow Museum and Art Gallery, 1980

Charles Rennie Mackintosh, Catalogue of Exhibition, Victoria and Albert Museum

Design in Education, Council for Art and Industry, 1937

The Embroideress, 1922–1939

Embroidery, edited by Mrs Christie, 1909

Embroidery, 1932–1939

Fancy Needlework, 1906–1955, Manchester and London

Glasgow School of Art – Annual Reports 1903–4, 1907–8

Glasgow School of Art, Session Prospectus, 1906

Hanging in the Choir of Wells Cathedral, Richard Henry Malden, Dean of Wells, 1948

The History of the Leek Embroidery Society, Keele University, 1969

Modern British Embroidery, Victoria and Albert Museum, 1932

Needlecraft, 1910

Needlecraft Monthly, 1907–1910

Needle and Thread, edited by Mrs Christie, 1914

The Needlewoman, 1919–1937

The Needlework Development Scheme, Glasgow – Origins and Aims, 1951

Stickerei-Zeitung, 1911–1914

Stickereien und Spitzen, 1919–1932

Stitchcraft Magazine, 1934–1936

The Studio, 1899, 1897–8, Autumn 1916

The Young Englishwoman, 1870–1874

The Young Ladies' Journal, 1886

Index

Figures in *italics* refer to illustration pages